Metamorphosis

From Cotton Picker
to Community Leader

by

James F. Daniels

To Pat

Best wishes

James Daniels

2/14/19

Metamorphosis – Cotton Picker to Community Leader, the autobiography of James F. Daniels

ISBN# 978-1537027487

Published by Armstrong Media Group, LLC
1655 N. Clyde Morris Blvd , Suite 1
Daytona Beach, FL 32117

armstrongmediagroup@gmail.com

Editors:
Michael A. Pyle, President of Armstrong Media Group, LLC
and
Veronica Helen Hart

Cover art and other services performed by Chris Holmes of Whiterabbitgraphix.com
Cover photo of James Daniels by Robert Hart

Dedication

To:

My father,
The Reverend Franklin Roosevelt Daniels

My mother, Marietta Dowdell Daniels

My wife, Carrie

and

My children Derek and Susan

Acknowledgments

I wish to acknowledge the following, many of who have been waiting anxiously for me to finish this book. Most are somehow related to my weekly volunteer work at Florida Health Care in Daytona Beach, Florida. I'd like to thank Karen Moore and her Volunteers at Florida Health Care, Melanie and a nice group of ladies in ophthalmology, Dr. Staley, Didi, Amy, Jackie, Pam, Karen, and the rest of the orthopedic gang, the pretty little doctor and her 320 building, Mark and his professional staff in pharmacy, Barb and her staff in pain free services, Dr. William and his group in cardiology, Linda and the smiley group in dental, my friends Kathy, Beth, Cindy, Hugh, Chip, Loretta, Bonnie, Laura, Christine, Barb and the x-ray gang, Jerry Lynn, B. D. B. , Kristin and her great staff in ultrasound.

Mt family Frank, Willie, Lele, Rodney, Peggy, Inez, Tot, Jerry, Bessie, Joe, Bernice, Lola, Geneva, Pastor Ed, Ellen, Verdia, Edna, Luther, Larry H. , Lonnie, Alma, Willie Mae, Myrle, Vilma, Mary Jane, Connie, Mary, Julia, Shirley, Kathy, Fields, Stewart, Jerry. Luther, Gwen, Debose, Ferrell, Tiffany and family, Sherrie Henry, Lee, Pat, Alice, Shirley, Mary Lou, Temple, The Turners, Arthur, Doris, the Blacks, the Greens, the Smiths, James, Denise, Holly, the lab group, Barbara and staff, Bonnie and the Holly Hill Auxiliary, Jeffery and Almeta, Alice, Edith, Roseanne, John and Ivory, Lisa, Bob, Dade, Dr. Oli family, Marie, Phil, Jimmy, Señorita, Alson, Devan, Lee and Janice.

I'd also like to thank the staff at Halifax Historical Society Museum, the Broxton family, my fellow Nuisance Abatement Board Members, The Historic Preservation Board Members, and Saint Timothy's Episcopal Church members.

The Publisher and the author give thanks to:

Deborah Shafer of the Volusia County Library System for suggesting that James F. Daniels and Michael A. Pyle work together as author and publisher, and her undying support throughout this project, which is certainly going to continue.

Professor Leonard "Len" Lempel, of Daytona State College for his overall support, publishing an excerpt in the Halifax Herald and writing an eloquent endorsement of this book.

The Halifax Historical Society, Daytona Beach, Florida, specifically including Fayne LeVeille, the Ormond Beach Historical Society, specifically including Suzanne Heddy, and Bill Dodson, for helping to find useful photographs and their overall support of this effort.

Ebony Nichols for her assistance in transcribing.

Veronica Helen Hart for transcribing major portions of the book, organizing, giving life to the words, editing, and uploading the final manuscript.

Chris Holmes of Whiterabbitgraphix.com for working on cover art, photographs and other services.

Metamorphosis

From Cotton Picker to Community Leader
James F. Daniels

One

1939 – Ormond Beach, Florida

I pulled the string. The light came on. Jerry pulled it, and the light went off. Dock took a turn. Then so did Bessie.

"That's enough. All of you." Aunt Lily Mae stood in the doorway of her bedroom, hands on her hips. "I'm right pleased to have you all here, but your uncle and I have to get to work in the morning. Now, settle down. You'd think none of you had seen an electric light in your lives."

She was right. We hadn't.

That night, my entire family, a couple of cousins, and aunts and uncles had arrived at my Aunt Lily Mae's house on Yonge Street. When she'd encouraged my parents to move to Ormond Beach, which is just north of Daytona Beach, I don't think she quite expected sixteen of us to arrive all at once. We rode into town packed into an ancient Model T Ford truck. My father had attached a body on the back of it, turning it into a very long, very large station wagon. The back end stretched way out past the back wheels, about as far as it was to the front wheels.

All sixteen of us were crammed inside that wagon, along with a few chickens. As many of our belongings as we could carry were inside or tied on the top.

Aunt Lilly Mae had fed us a delicious meal of fried fish, mashed potatoes and greens when we arrived. She'd poured water straight from a faucet into a pitcher. She'd opened what looked like an icebox, and put little pieces of ice into the pitcher. In Georgia, we sometimes bought a big piece of ice and put it in the icebox to keep things cold. Here, it was all backwards. The icebox was already cold, and the ice was used to make water cold.

I motioned to my brothers and sisters to follow me. "You won't believe this. They have this room right inside the house with something like a chair and water inside it. You don't have to go outside in the weather to that stinky outhouse anymore. When you're done going to the bathroom, you push this handle and water rushes in and cleans it right out!" I flushed.

"What?" exclaimed my sisters Rosetta, Lily, and Bessie in unison as they scurried in behind me and stuffed the room.

I pulled the handle of the faucet on the sink, and water flowed. I turned it off. "You can wash your hands right here."

My siblings vibrated with excitement.

"I can't believe this," Lily said. "Y'all get out so I can use it."

We boys went to explore further while Rosetta and Bessie anxiously waited outside the door.

Inez, the eldest at thirteen, acted casual, pretending to be unimpressed by all the new technology.

The littlest of our siblings fell asleep as soon as their heads hit their pillows, but most of the older kids buzzed for hours.

By midnight, the two-room house was littered wall-to-wall with people lying on pallets that we'd brought from Georgia. We called what we slept on pallets. They were made up of a quilt and a cotton-filled sack with a knot tied on one end; you'd sleep on one half and cover up with the other half. We also had a pillow for our heads, which was a flower sack stuffed with cotton or old clothes.

A couple slept in the station wagon, and a couple of the adults slept at Aunt Lilly's neighbors' home.

I lay on my pallet, eyes wide, imagining what else we'd experience in days to come.

Dock, my oldest brother, whispered all through the night. "Did you see the dishes? The glasses? The knives and forks? Their shoes? Their clothes. I want a job like our uncle got."

I whispered back, "They are rich. Maybe everybody here in Florida is rich."

It had never even occurred to me that anybody had sets of matching knives, forks and spoons, sets of plates that were all the same colors and patterns, and sets of drinking glasses.

In Georgia we had tin cans and tin pans. If we bought jelly, we'd have a glass jar to eat or drink from.

Aunt Lily Mae was my dad's sister. Every time she visited us in Cordele, she'd say, "Whyn't y'all come on down ta Ormond Beach, and get away from this place?"

My dad would say, "We doing all right here in Georgia but we'll think about it and let you know."

He said to our mom that he was afraid to bring all us young'uns to Ormond Beach, because he heard there was a big old ocean down there, with huge waves rolling towards shore. The biggest body of water we'd ever seen was the Flint River that runs through Georgia.

Aunt Lily Mae brought it up in every letter she wrote. Our dad finally gave in.

Our father had explained to some of us that Uncle Charlie earned a pretty good living working at John D. Rockefeller's mansion over on the beach side of Ormond Beach.

As our father put it, Aunt Lily Mae and Uncle Charlie were "doing all right."

This was the start of an amazing new experience for our family, once we got used to being out of bondage.

When Aunt Lily Mae and Uncle Charlie rose to leave for work at the Rockefeller mansion, "across the bridge," those of us who'd talked all night finally fell asleep.

The ruckus of everybody else rising a couple of hours later woke us. The girls waited in a long line to use the fancy toilet, so Dock and the rest of the boys snuck out into the back yard behind a small tree.

While Mother worked to put together some breakfast, she discovered she didn't have enough lard for the biscuits. As I was the nearest when she made this discovery, she caught me by my sleeve. "James, Aunt Lily says there's a store just across the railroad tracks. See your father for some money and get on over there for a container of lard. And don't dawdle. I need to feed a lot of hungry folk here."

I found my father at the rear of the line for the bathroom. He gave me a bunch of coins. "If you got a nickel left from this, bring back some candy for the little ones."

I went out the front door, and looked up and down the street. The railroad tracks were hardly a stone's throw away. The white clapboard building on the other side had a sign out front. I couldn't read it from where I stood, but I guessed it would be the store.

The kids who slept in the truck were just waking up.

"I'm going to the store. Want to come?"

They grumbled something which I took to be a no. At nine years old, I was feeling pretty brave, going across the tracks by myself.

The store was the front part of a house. When I reached it, I stopped. In Georgia, we couldn't go to the front of any white business. We either had to talk from a window, or they would have a door in the back or on the side, just for us. I kept looking for the door I could enter. I couldn't get to the rear of the building because it was blocked by a big fence. Where could the door for me to enter be? I couldn't just walk in the front door, could I? I finally went up on the front porch and stood by the front door, not sure what to do.

5

A white lady walked up behind me, pulled open the door and said, "Go right on in, sonny."

I dropped my head, terrified to look up at her. Back home, nobody could look directly at a white person, especially at a white woman. She stood there, holding the door.

I sheepishly stepped inside. The white lady followed me. "Morning, Louis," she said to a white man who was stacking cans of vegetables.

"Morning, Mrs. Miller." He turned to me. "What can I do for you, sonny?"

I directed my eyes to the floor. "My mother needs some lard and if I have enough money, I want to buy some candy."

He said, "Lard's over there."

I guessed he was pointing somewhere, but I was afraid to look. I kept my head down and scratched at it. "Yes, sir." I didn't move.

"Well, for pity's sake." He crossed the space and headed behind a big shelf near where the lady was picking things out.

He came back and set the lard on the counter. "Now, you go choose your candy. And, son, look at me when I speak to you."

I looked up as ordered. "Yes, sir." Then I dropped my head again. No white man had ever said such a thing to me. Whenever we had gone into the commissary at the plantation in Cordele, we weren't allowed to touch anything. We had to point or tell the shopkeeper what we wanted and he would go get it for us. We couldn't pick up a candy bar from a box. If we wanted something to wear, we could touch it, or pick it up, but never try any clothes on.

Once it registered that I could actually pick out my own candy, I went to where he pointed and took my time studying all the choices, then selected what I figured was the most I could get for a nickel and took it up there to the counter. He took my nickel and gave me a penny back. He passed the lard and candy over to me, and then, surprising me even more, he said, "Thank you, sonny."

I gulped and remembered my manners right quick. "You're welcome." I was so grateful, I backed out of the store saying, "You're welcome. You're welcome, sir."

I ran home and I told my mother what had happened. "There's a white man down at the store and he said 'Thank you, sonny,' and he let me go and pick up the candy that I wanted. I could pick it up out of the box all by myself."

She smiled and said, "Well, it's different down here, son."

Mom was sure right about things being different. Back home I lived with my family in one of sixteen shanties on the Sidney Wells Plantation in Cordele, Georgia. Our responsibility was to help grow the crops. We planted, cultivated and harvested watermelon, corn, sorghum, and rice. We also grew brown fuzzy-shelled velvet beans used to feed animals.

Slavery was over in Georgia, but on the plantation, we were basically indentured servants, which didn't feel much different from being a slave. The white man was the master, and we had few rights.

We had left Cordele, Georgia about six o'clock in the morning the day before to make the 240 miles journey. People in the towns we passed stopped to stare at us as if we were a parade. We must have been some sight with so many of us in that long, long, truck with all the bundles and chickens in and on it.

We had to make a lot of bathroom stops for the younger ones, and we had to stop for a meal or two. For me and my brothers and sisters, the move to Florida was an adventure; the stops a great picnic. While it was nothing but fun for us, I can't imagine how the grown-ups felt, crammed into that car with so many kids.

It was dark when we got into Palatka, Florida. We were about to cross the St. John's River when Dad saw the soldiers standing on the corners of the bridge. They looked like they were holding weapons–guns. He stopped the car. It took him a moment to recognize they were statues. The grown-ups chattered with nervous laughter, thinking it was the military about to stop us from crossing that bridge.

Later that day, our folks went out looking for a place for us to live. They located a little shack, which we were able to get, down by the railroad track. I'm not sure how my father worked it out because we had very little money, but we settled in that little house. It didn't have any water, but we were just about half a mile from the water works. Everybody that lived in those quarters could get water by going down to the water plant public works department. They had a faucet out in the middle of the yard. It was free for anybody who wanted to carry water back to their homes. This was another new adventure. We kids enjoyed the task because we didn't have to do anything but carry water.

Our new house had a little heater. Outside was a tank with a pipe that ran inside to the heater. All we had to do is turn it on and light a match and we had heat. This was like heaven. No chopping wood or making a fire, and no one had to get up early in the morning to work in the fields. We didn't know what to do with ourselves.

Two

Sidney Wells Plantation in Cordele, Georgia

I was born on the Sidney Wells Plantation in Cordele, Georgia, the fifth child, second boy, to Frank and Marietta Daniels on March 3, 1928. A midwife, driving a mule wagon arrived just in time to help with the delivery. My folks were pleased to have a boy, because boys meant another worker for the plantation.

Later, eight more children came along: Jerry, Bessie, Joe, Bernice, Iola, Edward, Geneva, and Lawrence. All fifteen of us, including our parents, were packed into our two-bedroom cabin.

My birth was recorded at the Crisp County courthouse. Back then, farm hands were not issued birth certificates. A member of the family submitted my name to a clerk at the courthouse, who wrote it by hand into the book. After a certain period of time, I figured the book probably faded and disappeared, but recently I've been informed that the record of my birth still exists.

Every cabin on the plantation had its own well

and outhouse. The outhouse was a little wooden shack over a big hole. Inside the outhouse was a big wide board with two holes—that was the seat. When that particular hole filled up, they dug another one beside it. Three or four guys picked up the outhouse, moved it over the new hole, and then covered the old hole. They kept moving it and moving it until it traveled all the way around from one end of the property to the other. They always tried to keep it as close as possible to the back door of the cabin so it wouldn't be too far to walk.

Our houses were built the same as the outhouses, with basic, unpainted wood, a tin roof and no glass for the windows. The one big difference was that the windows in the house had wooden shutters on hinges that we closed at night to keep the mosquitoes out in the summer and the cold out in the winter.

We had a fireplace in the living room and one bed right near it, where our mother and father slept. The two youngest children, Joe and Bernice, slept on pallets on the floor beside their bed. At night, my father put a big oak log in the fireplace, so the fire would burn all night. That fireplace kept the whole house warm, even the sole bedroom where Inez, Dock, Willie, Rosetta, Lillie, Jerry, Bessie and I slept, because the back of the fireplace protruded into it. The room had no beds; the children slept on the floor on pallets.

We kept the water on the back porch. The only dipper we owned stayed in that bucket of water, and everybody drank from it, night and day. When the water got low, someone went out to the well, a big hole in the ground, nothing fancy, and lowered the bucket to draw the water.

A little icebox stood out there, too, but was only used when we could get ice, about once or twice a month when we went into town to buy things that we couldn't get in the commissary.

The food was good; we enjoyed whatever we had. We planted a little garden in the back yard so we had sweet potatoes and turnip greens, which gave us the chance to have a few extra things. Quite a few people out there planted different things.

We'd get a slab of bacon and make it last as long as we could by cooking it in such a way so we could save the fat. We seasoned the greens and other vegetables that we ate with the grease from the pork.

We had a few chickens, too. It was a special treat to have chicken every once in a while. We had a few eggs, too, every once in a while. It was just a matter of being thrifty, smart, and doing things that helped.

We had one or two hogs. We couldn't have any more than that because the plantation owners didn't want us to have the ability to produce our own food. They wanted to sell us whatever we needed from their commissary.

The commissary was a store up at the big house, owned and operated by the plantation owner. They told us we farmhands could get everything we needed in the commissary, so we didn't need a whole lot of cash money. Every time anyone bought something, they wrote it down in a book, a tablet with everybody's name in it. They didn't miss a single sale.

They kept count of what was purchased because every September was payday, when they settled up with the farmhands. The head of each family presented himself and the owner told him how much they'd bought on credit during the year, and exactly how much they'd earned from their labor. A man was pleased if he came out of the hole, even if it was only for a short while.

A family could end up after the annual reckoning with anywhere between two and seven dollars. Far as I know, no one ever received as much as ten dollars for the year. The owner always commented something like, "You had a pretty good year, you cleared four dollars and eighty cents. " He gave the man the cash, then would tell him, "Saturday, you can use the mule and wagon to go into town."

Then the family drove into town to buy things they weren't able to get at the commissary, like an ice cream cone. Those cost a nickel, and if you chose a double, they gave two and a half scoops for ten cents. We kids always looked forward to that.

We were considered indentured servants, which was just like being slaves. We had no way to leave. If we needed to go into town, we had to get permission to use the owner's mule and wagon because we didn't have transportation.

If we got real sick, we had to go to the owner or the plantation boss and get a note to go into town. The doctor wasn't going to wait on us or do anything for us unless we had that note. We didn't have any money; we didn't have anything. It was rare to ask to see the doctor; a person had to be pretty sick. We had many home remedies that worked, so we didn't have a whole lot of need for doctors.

I did go there one time. The doctor's office was

a wooden building set up off the ground on stakes. Little steps led up to the backdoor. Inside, I sat on an old wooden bench and waited. Someone heard the door when it closed because after a while a nurse came to see who was back there. She didn't actually come into the waiting room. There was a little window which she could look through first. A little canning jar with some alcohol and a thermometer stood on a shelf under the window. She stuck that thermometer in my mouth. It was bitter stuff; I can all but taste it now. She asked, "What hurts you, boy?"

I could have said, "I got a stomach ache," or "My head hurts," made no difference because she wouldn't take our blood pressure or listen to our heart beat. She'd just stick that thermometer in our mouths and read it when it was ready. She would never touch us.

While I sat there, she went back into the office and told the doctor about me, and then returned in a little while and gave me a note. "Here, take this over to Miss Killebrew." Miss Killebrew's Grocery and Drug Store, everything combined, was about a block away.

"You go down there with this note and give it to them. Miss Killebrew will give you a little envelope of some pills."

I got my pills, not knowing if they were aspirin or not, but she told me to take one at morning and one at night. But she gave me those tablets and I went back out on the farm. The Owner would expect anyone who was sick to be well in the next few days.

Along with the tablets my mother would prepare our home remedy, which I believe did more good than those tablets. It was the same for all the families.

I never did see a doctor.

There might have been one or two black doctors, but the closest black doctor to us would have been in Atlanta. Even if they had set an office up in town, they'd starve to death because they would have no black clientele who could pay money to keep the office open. We had no money, and whites certainly wouldn't go to one of them.

Three

Rigby School, Ormond Beach, Florida

In Ormond Beach, Mom was all set to find out about sending us to the Rigby School, which was within walking distance from our house. That building is still there, and now houses the Pace School for Girls in Ormond Beach. Aunt Lily Mae told our mother we shouldn't even try to go to school until she got us some clothing to wear. She didn't want the teachers and students to think that we were what we really were, country hicks. She wanted us to be presentable, not the laughing stock of the campus.

The only pants we boys brought with us were overalls. Just like all males on the plantation, we always wore long johns under our clothes, no matter what the weather was like. I had a faded old shirt and a jumper, which was basically a jacket. For shoes all we had were worn out old brogans. We had caps. We needed them in the wintertime because it got powerful cold. As we got older on the plantation, we had to get up early in the morning and catch that mule out there.

We had on our brogan shoes and wool socks, overalls and long johns, and a leather cap with flaps on the side that buckled underneath the chin. It all came in handy when that wind was cutting.

On the Monday after we arrived, our aunt took my mother to a welfare office and told them what we needed in the way of clothing. They fitted us all up. We each came away with a couple of trousers and plaid shirts fit for city life. The welfare people also gave us some nice shoes and socks.

The girls were set with skirts and blouses, nice cotton socks, white cotton under-things, and shoes. All of us looked so clean and fancy.

Later on in the week, when we could dress up nice, we all went on to the school. The kids and the teachers, everybody, stood around looking at us. They must have heard about "them people from Georgia." The principal took us all into the chapel where we each met with a counselor who tried to determine our ages and how much we knew. She asked about the alphabet and questions that told her what level of academics we had reached in our limited Georgia schooling. She assigned us to different classes.

They put me in third grade because I could barely read. I felt like I was the biggest and dumbest person they ever had in the third grade. They said the teacher would work with me. Miss Lila Scott was the nicest teacher a person could ever meet. After the man in the store, she was the next person to make me feel like a human being. She said she was going to retire, but that before she finished with me that year I was going to be the president of the class and an A student. And that's what she did.

There was a cafeteria in the school where the whole family could eat for free. After eating, the kids would go outside to play until the bell rang to bring them back into classes. Instead of playing outside, I would work with Miss Scott after I finished eating. She dedicated herself to me. She'd read the lessons to me during those lunch hours, worked with me after school and, on Saturdays, had me come to her house. Some of the other teachers did the same for my sisters and brothers. She really took a lot of time with me and she taught me, so by the end of that first year I was doing just as well as or better than the other students. To give me a little bit of self-esteem, she appointed me as the president of the class. I didn't even know what a president was supposed to do, but she taught me that too.

I would not be where I am today if it weren't for Miss Lila Scott. When I went to school I couldn't read or write, she gave me the incentive to learn, taught me, trained me, and gave me the self-esteem to try and make something out of myself. After that, I was fortunate enough to be president of every class from third grade all the way through twelfth.

Although Rigby was a school just for blacks, we had all of the material and equipment that we needed. The school was named after the Ormond mayor's wife, Maude Rigby. Over the auditorium there was a big sign, Maude Lawrence Rigby Chapel. She and her rich friends often came to check on the school. We had a library and they saw to it that we had all the things we needed, which was really great. We had a wonderful start there.

Textbooks were a different thing, because we got used ones after the white schools were done with them. I'd always look inside the front cover of the books at the names of white students who'd used them before me. As I went from grade to grade, I got to know a lot of the white kids' names. In later years, when I met some of those white students felt I knew them already.

At the end of the tenth grade at Rigby, we received a diploma of graduation, because that was the highest grade offered to us. In the white schools, like Ormond Senior High, students had to go through twelfth grade before they got a diploma.

In 1948, after graduating from Rigby, I applied to go to college and learned that I needed a real high school diploma. There was one high school for blacks, on Campbell Street in Daytona Beach, about ten miles away. I began traveling on a raggedy old school bus to the area of Daytona Beach where only black people lived so I could finish eleventh and twelfth grades and receive my high school diploma.

During our early years in Ormond, Mom worked for the welfare agency along with a sweet, tiny, white lady named Miss Reed. Mom helped Miss Reed pack up baskets to be delivered to the poor, and of course we would get

James Daniels, 1948, High School Senior photo

one. Miss Reed was the only person we knew who would come pick up my mom when they delivered the baskets or did other errands. And Mom sat in the front seat with her.

My mother told us about the first time Miss Reed came to pick her up. When Mom opened the back door to get in, Miss Reed said, "Why are you sitting back there? I'm not going to chauffeur you. I don't bite."

My mother said, "I just thought maybe. . . "

After that, they became real buddy-buddies. Miss Reed used to come to the house. She talked with us and got to know us all. She helped out with our clothing. The welfare shirts we were given were not the stylish kind, but we appreciated them and we wore them. Some of the kids at school who knew would tease us about wearing the 'commodity shirts,' but that didn't bother us none. We didn't have any shame because of what we had gone through on the plantation in Georgia.

We got a lot of good things from the welfare office to help us along the way. We were doing pretty well between our own work and their help. We said there are some good white folks in Florida. They are nothing like those we had to deal with in Georgia in those years.

Four

School in Cordele, Georgia

I had gone to grammar school in Cordele, along with the others who were big enough, starting at the Morgan Grove Baptist Church. Miss Freddie May Nealey, who had finished sixth grade, was our teacher. She taught all ages, though she wasn't really particular about what age you were. She seated us according to our size. We only were in school about a total of three months during the year. At the end of each school year, they put on a little graduation ceremony with all the kids in all the grades. On a Saturday night, we'd get all cleaned up, and our parents would accompany us to the ceremony in the church. The kids stood at the front, and the parents sat on the benches. Each one of us kids had to recite something we'd memorized especially for this event.

One year, when I was about six or seven, my role was to hold a piece of two by four timber and say, "Campbell Soup can make me strong; I can hold this up all day long."

We had to plant the crop before we could attend

school. We would then have a month or so of schooling while the crop was growing. When it came time to harvest, school would be over so that we could work the crop.

For the cotton crop, we were called out as soon as the seeds started coming up, because we had to pull all the nut grass by hand so it wouldn't grow within the seedlings and hamper the crop. Nut grass was like a little weed with a nut on the bottom of it. Only the children would get on their hands and knees to yank out the nut grass.

While we young'uns did that, the grown-ups were sent down to pick velvet beans or work in the cornfield.

The plantation owner's son was our foreman. He was about sixteen years old. He rode his horse out every morning to give us our assignments.

"All you little niggerlets come over here and pull the nut grass."

We didn't know much about that word, because we only heard it there, working on the farm. We honestly didn't think anything of it. I guess it's because they didn't make it sound like a nasty invective when they said it. It seemed kind of matter-of-fact. We later learned it, as well as the word it was derived from, was a very hateful word.

We always enjoyed pulling the nut grass because there were a lot of kids, maybe ten or fifteen. We crawled down the row of cotton pulling out that nut grass. Those rows were about a mile long. Each one of us got a row, and we'd laugh and talk and have fun pulling up the nut grass from around the cotton plant. While the grown people were over doing other jobs, we could say whatever we wanted.

If we got thirsty and needed water, we had to get it from the keg which was kept at the end of the row. We ran to the end of the row to get a drink, and ran all the way back, because we didn't want to get behind the others.

We had to crawl fast to get our row done before the sun went down because the next morning we'd come back and start on another section. We were expected to perform, so we did.

Later on, shortly before my parents decided to move to Florida, we changed to a school in Vienna, Georgia, a little settlement that had a post office and the school, but not much else. The school had several teachers. There were about twenty-five of us who came from the sixteen shanties on the plantation, so we all walked together. We started out at six in the morning when it was still dark. It took us an hour or more to walk the five miles into Vienna. As we were walking down that road, the white kids would ride by on a bus on the way to their school. When we heard a noisy, old bus coming down the road, about to pass us, we hopped over the ditch into the pecan orchard until it went by, because whenever it passed us, those white kids threw things at us and called us names.

But one day, after the longest time of trying to avoid the bus, with no warning or explanation, someone threw old toys out the windows of the bus. They also tossed out packets of soda crackers and even sometimes clothes. We collected what they threw. From then on, every day, the bus would slow down as they reached us, and they'd throw out different good things. We never had to jump into the ditch again.

The kids no longer called us names. That was quite a change from the way it was at the beginning. I guess they had a change of heart, but when we got to the school the teachers still poked fun at us. They called us country hicks.

We always carried our lunch, using a syrup bucket as our lunch box. Most of the time we brought biscuits, fried fatback, and syrup to pour over it.

We had a lot of country habits. If we had a cold, we'd wear a talla rag. It was like a bib, dipped in beef fat (hot lard) worn under our clothes, right next to our skin. It was very greasy and would soak into our shirts. The idea was that we would not get too sick or catch pneumonia if we wore the talla rag. It seems to have worked because we were healthier than some of the kids in town.

The other thing that we did for health sake was to wear an asphidity bag. A paste of ginseng, pokeweed, yellow root, and I don't know what else, was stitched into a little bag to wear nestled in the hollow at the lower part of the neck. The odor was so strong, so they believed it would keep the wearer from breathing in any germs. Anyway, nobody wanted to be too close to that smell, so maybe that's why we didn't get sick as much as the others.

Well, we looked like bums and smelled bad, too.

Five

Early Childhood in Cordele

I must've been about six or seven years old when I was baptized. All of us candidates gathered about 9 o'clock or so on a Saturday morning, and we'd go down to the Drayton River, a little river in Drayton, a small settlement out on the highway that goes from Vienna, Georgia to Americus.

We had to carry a cloth or towel to dry off afterwards, and a change of clothes. The deacons stepped into the water first and pushed back the shrubbery so we could get down to the water. Some of the deacons batted at water moccasins with sticks while the preacher dipped us in the water. Now that I think about it, it was a pretty dangerous undertaking because those moccasins are poisonous.

We had a lake down there where we used to go in the afternoon to catch fish, mostly without any fishing poles, just a line with a lead on it and a cork to hold it up, a hook, and bait. We tied the line to a stick and shoved the stick into the side of the bank and then left it, sometimes overnight. The next morning we would snatch it up to see how many fish we caught. Usually we had something, because the fish were just as hungry as we were. We didn't have much problem catching fish; we pretty much put anything out there and they ate it.

We also caught fish by mudding the pond. My grandfather once told me he'd done it with his own father and grandfather. On a Saturday afternoon, we'd gather up our garden rakes, hoes, sometimes a stick, and walk out into the little pond in the middle of the field located on the plantation. We walked as far out as we could and scraped and dug into the bottom until the mud was all stirred up so the fish surfaced to get some air. As they popped up we caught them in a big cloth sack. When it was filled with fish, we let the water settle back down and left the rest of the fish until the next time.

That Saturday night, several families got together for a real fun time; a fish fry outdoors.

Usually our fryer was the wash pot, the same pot we boiled our clothes in. It had three legs and sat up on bricks. The cooks put a lot of fat, shortening, or oil into the pot, and let it get real hot for frying. Others made music while the rest of us danced. We called it a frolic.

We turned a tin tub used for washing the clothes upside down. The man with the best rhythm used sticks and played it like a drum. Another one ran a wooden clothes-pin up and down the corrugated metal laundry scrub board following the pattern of the drummer.

Somebody else would pluck on strips of rubber from an old inner tube stretched between two number ten cans. It sounded a bit like picking a guitar.

A couple of marbles inserted through a little hole in the side of a dried-out vegetable shaped like a squash—long neck with a round bottom—made another instrument that could be shaken to the rhythm of the tin tub.

We danced late into the night.

We didn't have sodas, beer, or wine, but every once in a while somebody would sneak in a little *buck*, a drink made from fermented sugar cane grown by a man down the road a little ways. He squeezed the juice out of the cane, grinding the cane stalks between two big metal wheels turned by a mule walking in a circle pulling a long shaft attached to the grinding wheels.

He boiled the juice in a big metal vat over a fire. As it boiled, foam came to the top. We scraped it off and put it in a barrel right beside the vat, getting all the foam and the impurities out of the juice. What was left was nice sugar cane, pure delicious sugar cane. We let the foam sit in the barrel and ferment, and the bees would get at it and help it along.

After a few weeks, it became very clear with a crust over the top of it. Because the barrel was just left open, a few bugs and critters would also be floating around on the top but we scraped that off and got down in there and it was pretty clear, perhaps just a little murky. This is what we called *buck*. Since it was during the hard of winter, it was good and cold and you could take a drink of that and feel like a millionaire for a little while.

We put the hard crust scrapings in the trough that the hogs ate out of. Then we really had some fun because the hogs had a good time when they ate it. They got all dizzy and drunk just like a lot of the people who drank that *buck*.

We children, even younger than ten years old, were known to have a little buck once in a while. So it was a good time for all of us.

The real syrup was bottled in half gallon or quart buckets, but we weren't allowed to sell any syrup in town. If somebody came out to the mill, and they wanted a little bottle, you could give it to them or sell them some.

White business people bought the syrup the country people brought in, canned it up properly, put the labels on it, and marketed it. They shipped it out to sell all over the country because it was pure good quality syrup. They paid the farmers pennies and were able to make dollars.

When a farmer came up with an idea to grow something different, he'd share it with the others. Some had a little watermelon patch and they could sell a few. We could sell some of our products at the plantation, but it was not legal for us to take them to market. The white merchants would come to the fields to buy the products, and then take them to the farmers' market, where they had a booth. Anyway, we didn't have transportation to take our products to market. The ones who might have a car or a truck or some kind of an old raggedy piece of equipment wouldn't have gas to run it. They might be able to get a quarter's worth of gas, or fifty cents' worth at the most, to make little trips in the countryside, but the plantation owners controlled the gasoline for their vehicles.

My grandfather told me about things that happened during these get-togethers in his day.

Grandpa's Story:

"While everyone was frying fish, playing music, and having a good time on Saturday night, some white men might

My grandparents in front of their house in Cordele.

come down their way. Our people stopped the music and everyone became awful quiet, not sure what they wanted, what they were going to say or who they were coming to get. Most of the time it turned out they were coming to get girls. They'd just come in and pick out the best-looking girls and take them away with them. They kept them for two or three hours—sometimes the rest of the night, before they turned them loose and let them come back. A lot of them became pregnant.

"Some girls became regulars of certain men, who then provided them with their own shacks to live in. Thelma was one of the most beautiful girls I ever saw. She was a favorite. Some of the white wives knew when their husbands had a baby with a slave so they did more for them than the others. Most of the time they gave them a job working around the big house, either keeping the garden or cleaning.

"These children of slave owners and later plantation owners benefitted by having universities created just for them. They might be called "traditional black" colleges now, but they were for the sons of those rich white men.

"After the Emancipation Proclamation, the slave owners' children were sent to agricultural and mechanical colleges in all of the southern states. That's why they have Florida A&M, Alabama A&M, Texas A&M. Later, those colleges were for regular black children, but owners' offspring would now go to the nicest colleges, like Xavier, Fisk, Atlanta, and Howard."

Our nighttime fun was to us, as well as our forefathers, top-notch entertainment. Of course we didn't have anything at that time to compare it with. The only difference between us in the days I was young and my forefathers when they were my age was that they were in slavery and we were in indentured servitude.

On Sunday mornings, we had to get up pretty early because it was quite a walk to the church. We had Sunday school, morning service, and another service in the evening. We stayed there all day because it was too far to walk back home between services. There was only one church and everybody was Baptist. We didn't know much about any other denomination.

An hour before we had to be there, a bell rang. We could hear the bell a mile away. The second bell ringing meant you should already be at the church. It was also rung to call people to a special meeting that meant something was going on or something had to be discussed. The bell was instrumental in helping us communicate.

Each church had its own cemetery right in back of the church, and it's still that way even today. They had family plots out there. It wasn't the matter of having to buy a plot, if a family had been attending that church for a certain period of time, they were entitled to be buried in that cemetery right behind the church.

In between the services, we'd go out in back of the church where there were benches for eating, like a picnic. Everybody spread out what they brought to eat. The deaconesses were the cooks in the kitchen. They had that big old woodstove going and fried up food for the people. Sometimes, when somebody brought some, they'd cook fish.

If someone brought a chunk of ice and lemons from town, we would have cold lemonade with our dinner after church, a real delicacy.

Sundays were happy times. We would never miss church. It was one of the few things we looked forward to. My biggest problem was walking home at night, so tired after a long day.

There were very few trees or bushes on the plantation, just a great big open area of farmland. Sometimes, after we harvested all the crops and there was nothing to keep the sand down, the wind would blow up a sandstorm. We'd cover our faces with handkerchiefs and scarves, but it still got into our eyes and noses. Whoever was in the house closed the shutters and covered the gaps with sheets or blankets.

But the wind-blown sand would find its way into the crevices.

My childhood occurred during the depression. That coupled with the fact we were farm workers out on a plantation made it even harder than for others.

Many times, the only thing we had to eat was corn meal and grits. We'd take a bag of corn up to the mill. The miller would take one fourth of it and dump it into his bin. He then ground the other three fourths into meal and grits. My father usually told him to give us two-fourths meal and one fourth grits.

As for cooking cornmeal cakes, because my mother didn't have the fat or oil to keep the bread from sticking, she sprinkled some of the corn meal on the hot frying pan instead. When she was ready to flip a cornmeal cake, she sprinkled more of the meal, so once again it would not stick. In the meantime she boiled the grits and we would eat grits and have a piece of corn bread to go with it.

My dad and some of the other men on the farm sometimes hunted at night for possums and raccoons. This made for happy times because we would clean the opossums well, boil them for a while, take them out and put them in the oven covered with red pepper. If we had a sweet potato, my mother would slice it and put it in the pan with the opossum. She'd cook the possum to a golden brown with those hot peppers and sweet potatoes. That was some real first class eating.

Of course, if you don't have a taste or an appetite for that type of thing, you may not like it. But, whatever my mother could get to cook, we ate, whether it was birds, possums, or rabbits.

Every once in a while the men would get a wild hog. That drew a lot of attention. Before roasting him, he had to be properly dressed, that is removing all the insides, and then take all the hair off. They would dig a trench, set the hog down, and set a fire. They'd put the hot coals on one side until that got done; then they would roll him over, alternating sides, until he was cooked all the way through.

It was always a great occasion. Once it was cooked everybody who was in hollering distance could share in the eating.

We loved to eat chitlins, which we considered a delicacy. They were actually the intestines of the hog. We cooked up those chitlins with rice and sweet potatoes. That was a special Sunday meal almost as special as fried chicken, rice, and collard greens.

When we killed the hogs, we also kept the bladder, dressed it down, and blew it up. We'd have a balloon that would last a long time. With a string attached to it we would have a good time watching it blowing in the wind from the back porch. We even would go around to other houses to see if they had more than one bladder. When they dried out, we painted pictures on them. Out on that farm, we didn't have toys or anything, so it didn't take much to make us kids happy.

Another thing we did was to cook the pig fat real good till we got all of the grease out of it; then, we would change pots and fry the meat. It's what they called cracklins, the fat meat that had been fried off a lot. You can eat the cracklins right then or, better yet, you could save them because they would not spoil.

We all also enjoyed sweet potatoes. Once they became ripe for harvesting, we dug them up, set them into piles in the sun and let the dirt dry them thoroughly. Then we wiped them off and cleared a spot on the ground in the back yard. We'd level it off nice and smooth, spread pine needles to make a cushion for them, and stack the sweet potatoes as high as we could reach. After that, we stood dried corn stalks leaning into the potatoes like a pyramid. Then we wrapped paper or old cloth around the stalks to form a nice enclosure that would protect the potatoes from the animals and the weather and covered it in dirt, just leaving a little hole in the front so you could reach your hand in there and retrieve a sweet potato when you wanted it. We'd create a little gate to keep the animals from going in. That's where we kept our sweet potatoes all year, in our sweet potato bank.

We moved from plantation to plantation during my childhood. The next farm I remember being on, it seems like we didn't stay there but a minute. They didn't grow anything but peanuts. We ended up with everything from peanut butter to peanut candy.

When it came time for the harvest on the peanut farm, a man with a mule plowed the peanuts up. We followed the plow, collected the peanuts, shook the dirt off, gathered about four or five bunches of them and stacked them in several piles right beside the row. A guy came along with a post-hole digger, dug a hole for a post and nailed two slats across the post, low to the ground, just high enough to keep the peanuts off the dirt.

We laid the peanuts on the slats, stacking them up as high as we could reach. Then the taller children and the grown-ups stacked more right up to the top of that pole going all the way round and when they finished, it looked like a Christmas tree. It was quite an artistic thing, but it was also functional. We left the peanuts, along with all the vines, in the sun for a few days to dry. The leaves wilted and died, leaving the peanuts, which then were hauled into town to the dealer. They stripped the peanuts off of the vine, washed them, and shipped them out, all over the country.

Once they were taken for processing, we could take as many as we wanted from what was left. We all ended up with two or three pockets full of peanuts to take home at night. We boiled the green ones. A lot of times we collected field peas and boiled them. By the time they were about halfway cooked, we shelled the peanuts and put them in the pot and they finished cooking together. When they were done cooking, we had a fine meal.

Many a night we had that for dinner because we ate what we had. It wasn't a situation where we could eat what we wanted.

We lived on one plantation that only grew peaches in a great big old orchard. That was Brown's farm. The good thing about picking peaches was that we could take all the ones that had fallen on the ground home with us. Boy, those were the best and sweetest ones, because they were fully ripe. We had peach pie, peach cobbler, and peach juice and anything else we could make out of peaches. During that time, we had a cow, so we also had milk to go with the peaches.

Cordele was the closest town to the plantations. We would go into town some Saturdays. The children didn't always go in, just grown folk mostly, except when Dad got a little settlement in September he'd take us with him and get us some ice cream and maybe some cheese and crackers—stuff that we hadn't been eating.

We had a certain section of town down there where all of the wagon train people came in from the country and we all got together, meeting on 12th Avenue. They called it The Bottom. They came with their mules and wagons and bragged about what they did, how their watermelons were, how good their corn was, and about what they were able to grow. Some of the men would slip off and go round to Riley Robinson's place. He was a black man who sold cookies, wine, beer, and a little moonshine on the side. We could go in there and get a hot dog, a hamburger, a pint of wine, or a beer. Half a pint of wine cost 20 cents. The prices were right because he had to keep them down to suit his clientele. He knew we didn't have much money; he got whatever we had.

Then there were the others who didn't have to buy liquor because they had their own moonshine still somewhere back in the woods. You could see the smoke rising over the woods for quite a distance.

The revenue man who came in from Atlanta always called the sheriff ahead of time and told him when he would be coming through. The sheriff would notify the moonshiners that the revenue man was coming on a certain day. They would take down the moonshine set up and put it in a shed until the revenuer came by and checked. He came with a deputy sheriff who took him around and showed him where he thought the moonshiners had their still.

To satisfy the revenue man, somebody would leave one of the stills standing, so at least he would have one to report and bust up. They thought that the sheriff was doing a good job, but in two days they were back running full force.

The revenue man returned every three to four months to check, but never caught anyone to put in jail because the sheriff always notified the moonshiners in advance.

When I was a young boy, gypsies came down the plantation's main road, four or five wagonloads in a group. Sometimes they had cows trailing them from place to place. They stopped overnight in a vacant lot then moved on, searching for better conditions.

One day a gypsy sold my uncle a mule. The mule looked fat and healthy, and that gypsy told my uncle what a good strong mule he was, so my uncle gave him six or seven dollars for the mule. The gypsies left. About four or five days after they had gone, the mule started acting sick. The veterinarian came by and said the mule had some type of worms and it was a matter of days before it would die. Come to find out the mule was just about to die when the gypsy sold it. My uncle was upset when the mule up and died a few days later.

The gypsies didn't respect our people like they did the white folk. So my uncle and some of these boys, neighbors and friends took it on themselves to look for those men and to try and get his money back. They went across the Flint River on over to Americus, Georgia.

They caught up with the gypsy and told him the mule had died. They explained what the veterinarian had told my uncle and said that the gypsy had to know it was sick when he sold it to him. My uncle told the gypsy he wanted his money back. The gypsy man looked at the black man and all the other black men standing beside him with sticks. He gave him his money back.

My uncle came home and told us, "The gypsy man gave us our money back. He thought we was gonna beat him up."

He may have got his money back after the man sold him a bad mule, but there were a lot of deals that happened with my family and other people on the plantation that were unjust, and there was nothing we could do about it because there was no law to help us. We couldn't sue anybody because we had no money. And if we'd had any money, we wouldn't have been out there in the first place.

Six

Work and Life on the Plantation

The plantation owners were pretty much the judge and the jury over everything, even whites against whites. They had great big houses, those rich white people. They owned everything. The owners paid the judges, the lawyers and everyone else, so those folk sworn to uphold the law pretty much worked for them and they told them exactly what to do. Blacks didn't own any property. We had no taxes; we had no voice; we couldn't vote. We were nobodies; we didn't count for anything. There were a lot of us out there, but we were the unheard majority. The poor white ones were kind of like us; they never had a chance either.

Something that still puzzles me now, though it didn't at the time because I didn't question it, was why the owners made it very clear that black friends, or even a black husband and wife, couldn't show too much affection for each other around white ladies. Now white men in the old days could come to our frolics and take away our black girls, and in current days could still take advantage of our black girls, but a couple of black people couldn't be seen hugging or being sociable in front of the white ladies on the plantation.

One thing was strictly forbidden; no black man could make eye contact with a white lady. If she was talking with him, he was supposed to look down, look around, scratch his head, doing something else, but no eye contact. This was strictly a no-no.

When I was working on the farm, a lot of times some of the guys would get in the mood and sing. That was also definitely forbidden. The plantation owners thought it was to tempt some of the white females. We were cautioned by our older relatives, "If you want to whistle while you work, you better be down at the other end of the row, not near the big house. Make sure you're out of hearing distance, and even if you are far away, you'd better not whistle or sing any song that's lovey or sexy like that."

There was an unwritten law that the black men couldn't wear tight fitting clothes, everything had to be loose, we couldn't wear clothes that would show our body's build; no white person should be able to see a black person's physique. Some of those guys had big muscular bodies, which they had to be even more careful to cover, so they wouldn't give the impression they were trying to tempt the white females. The uniform of the day consisted of denim overalls, a one-piece garment with a bib and straps that went over the shoulders. That had to be loose fitting. We also had a jumper, which was what we called the jacket worn over the overalls, made from the same material.

Joseph, a neighbor of ours, was a large, well-built, muscular man. One day, out in the field, Joseph got real hot. We didn't have shorts and nice undershirts; we wore our long johns under our clothes year round. He took off his jacket and went back out in the field, and it just so happened that one of the white ladies riding by on a horse saw him.

The story goes that she went and reported what she'd seen and as she described, "the one with big biceps," she seemed to be a bit excited, which angered her husband.

He headed out to the field and saw Joseph with his jumper off. Even with his long johns covering him, his muscular physique was evident. The white man confronted him. "What are you doing with your jumper off? You trying to tempt our white women? I ever catch you with your jumper off, you're going to be one sorry boy."

Joseph said, "It was hot out, and I'm way back here in the field. I didn't expect anybody to see me."

As he tried to explain, the man said, "Don't you give me any lip," and then he slapped Joseph across the face. Knowing he could do nothing about it, Joseph turned his back to walk away.

At that point the man kicked him. Angered, Joseph whirled around so quickly his head slammed into the man's jaw, cracking it, and knocking him out. Terrified of what he'd done, Joseph took off, running through the woods, trying to get far away from the plantation before the man woke up and gathered a posse to search for him.

He was able to escape through the woods, but there was a pond out there. He couldn't go much further because he heard them coming after him in their trucks. He knew they would really do him in if they caught him. So he got a reed, it looked kind of like bamboo, cut off a piece, and jumped in the pond. When he got in the pond he held the reed real tight in his mouth and held his nose. By doing that, he could stay under water for hours. He just had to be careful to make sure the tip of it remained above the water.

The white men searched everywhere in those woods and around that pond and finally gave up. Later on that evening they reorganized and searched elsewhere for him.

When Joseph was sure they were gone, he came out of the water and made it out to the roadside hoping to get a ride. When he heard the more ragged sound of a car, he jumped back into the bushes, but if he heard a nice smooth running car coming, then he would jump out in the road. He felt pretty sure it was people coming through from Ohio, and those Ohio people traveled in nice looking, smooth running cars. They would always be going to Florida or somewhere down in South Georgia.

Finally one of the Ohio people came by and they stopped. He told them what had happened. They gave him a ride down to Jacksonville where he felt pretty safe. He changed his name and eventually he and some of his relatives migrated to Daytona, where I became reacquainted with him and met his grandson.

We worked twelve hours from sun up to sun down whether we were on the plantation or not. Every once in a while one of the guys would pretend to be sick. It didn't happen too often because if you didn't work, you didn't eat. You had to have some kind of way to eat because you weren't getting any pay from the commissary.

If a man lingered too long, the plantation owner would become suspicious and let him know, "You don't want to work? That's fine by me. I'll send you someplace where you can be fed and be taken care of. And you'll have plenty of work." Though it seems hard to believe now, all the man had to do was tell the judge the worker stole something and next thing you know he'd be on a chain gang, because he was a prisoner.

The chain gang was a group of incarcerated fellows who had chains around their legs, all linked together, working on the roads. They kept the ditches cleaned out and the bushes cut near the roadside and anything else the powers-that-be saw fit for them to do. And the feeding was just as likely to be bread and water, nothing more.

A man could be sent to jail or sent to the chain gang for any number of things, such as staring at a white woman, or talking back to the boss. Little things like that could get you incarcerated. Folks didn't always go out on the chain gang, but they could be in jail for a few days. There was no looking at television in jail. Prisoners were always working. There was always plenty of work to be done around the city or inside the jail house—washing windows, cleaning, cutting yards, painting.

It was not a nice thing to be incarcerated during those times. If for some reason someone stole a chicken because his family was hungry, it was automatic jail time. This was one of those things that was inhumane.

If we did something, not necessarily even on our own plantation, but maybe on a Saturday while walking over to another plantation, or when we were having a ball game, and that something was not acceptable to the plantation owner, all he had to do was say what we did was wrong. His word was gospel. We would have to suffer the consequences.

We had to mind our Ps and Qs. As long as we were on anybody's plantation, they had control over us. It didn't matter who it was; if they were white and if they said it, they were right. We could be innocent, but we still couldn't defend ourselves. We had no defense.

We could always say, "I didn't do it." But then if we said that often and loud enough, the person making the accusation would say, "So you're calling Mr. or Miss So and So a liar," and that was just as bad as if we had admitted it. The best way out of any situation was to keep quiet, be humble, and ask for mercy. We'd say, "I won't do it no more," even though we didn't do it in the first place.

That's the way it was. Cumbersome as life was, we still enjoyed it, because we had nothing to compare it with. We thought everyone lived like us and didn't have any more than we did.

We were comfortable in our ignorance.

Seven

Social Security and Smoke House

In '34 or '35 the government announced a plan to take a penny out of every dollar anyone earned or received whatever way. Anybody who got a dollar figured on having to give Uncle Sam a penny out of that dollar. Didn't matter how anyone got it, he'd have to give a penny. That was the new law.

People got all up in arms, the whites and blacks. They came around to our shanties and said, "If any government folks come around and ask you to sign Yes for this new law, you say No and put your X by No."

The folks explained it to us this way "We don't want them to take a penny out of each of our dollars. They claim they'll save it for us until we retire. How are they going to keep up with the number of pennies we put in?"

They added that the government said they would do it anyway. "Look how many pennies you'll put in; they're going to give the white folks most of that money when they retire and you'll only get a little bit, so don't sign their paper."

That was Social Security they were getting all worked up over. They got so excited over this, they talked about forming a "mulecade" to go to Atlanta and protest to the governor about it.

They were about as upset about Social Security starting as they'd be now if the government tried to discontinue their checks.

This was later on when the depression was lightening up a little bit after Roosevelt was elected. Hoover had been president of the United States when it was really, really tough, when we were living on another plantation.

After Roosevelt was elected president in the early thirties, things started changing. He came out with the CCC Camp; that's where the big boys had the opportunity to go off into something like the military with uniforms, but mostly they would go out and help preserve the forest.

As the years went on, we were able to improve our conditions. Moving up from the indentured servant position, we were able to get a house on the plantation. My dad had constantly asked the plantation owner about a bigger house because there were nine of us. So finally he made a new arrangement with us and we got a bigger house down on the end of the plantation.

Our father also made an arrangement for better pay. Instead of paying us once a year and deducting commissary purchases, they began paying us once a week, so we had to pay cash at the commissary. That completely different arrangement made us a little bit more independent and flexible. If I remember correctly, my dad got a dollar a day, and the older of the children received fifty cents.

It reached a point that they allowed our family members to do outside jobs, because as the owners brought in new equipment they didn't need as many hired hands as before. We had more of a flexible schedule. Overall, that was a better arrangement because we were able to buy a cow, and we could have a few chickens. We were doing much better than we had been, but still we couldn't leave the farm unless we got permission from the plantation owner to use his wagon to go into town. There were still restrictions that were placed on us.

As time went on, we built a little smoke house out the back. When we killed a hog, we would make meat out of it and make sausage and we would have ribs and back bone. Then all we had to deal with was the ham, which we smoked in the smoke house. We would also smoke the bacon. Out of that hog we got sausage, bacon, and ham. We had something to eat, and we were able to share with our relatives and friends.

We had a nice little milk cow. During the day if we wanted some milk we could go out with a glass or can and milk us some milk, and then carry it back to the house and get us some cornbread and mash it up in the milk. That was pretty decent eating, milk and bread.

Our cow was tied up not too far from the railroad tracks. One day maintenance people from the railroad company came through spraying a poison to kill the grass and weeds alongside the track. Our cow got into some of that grass. They tried to save it, but we ended up losing the cow.

My father was grateful to get forty dollars the railroad company paid for the cow. That helped to get an old maroon colored Buick with a rumble seat we could open so a couple of people could sit in the back. It gave us a mode of transportation, but it was still an expense because it took gas and burned a lot of oil and had to have tires. So it was a job itself to have a car. We couldn't do much driving because we didn't have money to put gas in it. Most of the time it stood under a shade tree.

The tires on it weren't very good; we patched and fixed them from pieces of horse and mule harnesses. There was a substance like rubber on the back bands and belly bands which kept the harness chains from hurting the horses. It was like a rubberized cloth. When we needed to patch tires, we'd cut pieces off—we called the pieces "boot." We'd put glue on the inner tube and stick the boot to it, put the tube inside the tire and prop it up real tight to hold it in place, and keep it from leaking. Most of the time, it leaked anyway.

Eight

Family Work In My High School Years

I enrolled at the Campbell Street High School in Daytona Beach for my final two years of high school. I still worked a part-time job and I was the president of the eleventh and twelfth grades, thanks to the leadership skills and confidence Miss Scott instilled in me, which also helped me in later life.

All the kids in the family who were old enough had jobs to help support the family during our school years. We also all learned to save for the future. When we were younger and our daddy gave us each a dime to spend, we'd spend a nickel for candy and save the other.

When we first moved to Ormond, in thirty-nine or forty, just before the war started, life was pretty rough. My oldest brother got a kitchen job at the ocean-front Coquina Hotel, in Ormond Beach. He'd come home and tell us, "You should see all of the food they throw out. Some of those people will eat one little piece off their steak or pork chop. When it comes back to the kitchen, the guy there throws everything in the garbage can. All that good meat right in the can."

Every morning and afternoon, trucks brought the garbage from all the hotel kitchens to the west side of the river and deposited it on a huge mound at the end of the street in our neighborhood. Our family, other neighbors, even some white people living near us, went through the garbage and grabbed what still seemed edible.

Our brother told us that some of the waiters knew we foraged for food, so they tried to keep the better food clean by wrapping it in newspaper. The biggest problem we had with the general garbage was it was always mingled with used coffee grounds. We'd pull out big old hunks of meat, and wash and re-cook them. It was no shame we ate out of the dump during these rough years.

Life in Ormond, even digging in garbage, was far superior to what we'd experienced on the plantation.

As time went on, things improved. Dad cut wood at the sawmill just across the railroad track from our house in Ormond. He'd bring home scraps of wood where they'd removed the bark. He made good money cutting it up, and selling firewood. With almost all the kids working and our Dad selling firewood and also making a wage at the mill, we were doing real, real well.

Dad decided that, in addition to these ventures, he should buy an old trailer and start a little grocery store. It was kind of like a little 7-11 on wheels. He did pretty well with that, but it was mostly kids buying candy bars and sodas. We all took turns operating the traveling store, mostly in the afternoons and evenings, and on weekends. It wasn't a big operation, but it lasted for a while, along with the firewood business. It was a good experience for us and taught us some business sense.

My brother Dock was drafted into the army. That helped a lot because he sent his allotment to the family. This was when we started really enjoying our life. Our father was able to get a real car and we were able to move into a better house closer to the downtown area, and away from the cheaper houses by the railroad tracks.

The owners didn't want to sell to us because they weren't sure they'd be paid. We needed to pay on an installment basis. But they finally agreed. The total price was something like fifteen hundred dollars, spread out in monthly payments. The house was small for so many people. We couldn't possibly have our own rooms. We started adding on rooms and we kept adding. Eventually we got running water and nice bathrooms. We felt rich then. We had a car. We had electric lights. We could cook and eat. We had groceries.

So really it was just like heaven. For the first time in our lives we had a place we could call our very own. We planted gardens in the back and pretty little flowers in the front. We had plenty of time on our hands at that time, as opposed to when we were in Georgia working in the fields from sunup to sundown, five and a half days a week.

We continued to try to improve our living conditions. As the kids grew up and got jobs, so more money was coming in, we developed a family tradition that when anyone got paid he or she brought their money to the dining room table. Everybody knew exactly what each person earned. After we counted it, our daddy would take possession of it, and give us our spending money.

I was playing marbles with some of the neighbor boys one day and told them how we dealt with the money.

This one kid, Jeffrey, looked surprised. He said, "No, you're supposed to keep your own money. You worked for it."

I told him, "No, my Daddy says he furnished us with room and board, and he struggled for us, so we all combine it."

Jeffrey tried to convince me that I should be allowed to buy my own clothes and spend my money the way I wanted, but that was not the way we were taught. We were brought up to respect our parents and it worked very well for us.

The first year I was in school in Ormond, I had a newspaper route and did yard work in the neighborhood. When I was twelve, I helped a plumber building septic tanks. These septic tanks were far different from our outhouses up in Georgia. It might seem I was too young to be doing that kind of work, but I was big for my age—about as big as I am now—and no one asked me about it. To build a septic tank, we'd first dig a big hole, line it with blocks dividing the tank in two sections joined only by an overflow hole, then enclose it with a lid and seal it. All the waste went into the first section where anaerobic bacteria consumed everything. By the time it crossed over the partition into the second tank it was clear water, which then flowed into a dry well. This was a great big hole filled with rocks covered in felt paper, similar to roofing felt. The liquid in the dry well gradually soaked into the ground. As a result the septic tank lasted a long time, even with a lot of use.

If it did back up, then we had to go in, clean it out, reseal it, and start the process all over again. I worked on a lot of them. There were only two of us who dug septic tanks so we made pretty good money. I'm sure the business owner made a lot more than the workers, but I did all right. I was pleased to be getting big bucks to contribute to the family earnings.

There's an area north of Ormond Beach called Favoretta. There were a lot of pine trees there. We cut the trees down and sawed them up into about eight-foot pieces for pulpwood. My daddy had a great big old circular pulp wood saw. It looked something like a wheelbarrow with a saw on the front end. The motor sat on top of the 'handles' and a plastic belt went down to a pulley on the saw. After cutting, we laid the pieces of wood crossways on the frame our Dad had built on the back of a truck.

The Florida East Coast Railroad freight train left a couple of boxcars on the sidetrack in another nearby area called Espanola. We'd unload the truck on the boxcars. Once we filled a boxcar, which generally took about a week, we put up a sign and the railroad would send somebody to check it, close it up and seal the door. Then they paid us. Dad made pretty good money because we were all working for him. The railroad hauled the boxcar to the pulp wood factory in Panama City or Palatka, or more often to Jacksonville.

On some of those bigger pines, we'd cut an upside down V shape on the tree, nail a little metal box to below it and let the resin run right down into the cup. We checked each morning to see how much had deposited. If there was a measurable amount, we would pour it into a barrel. That's where we got turpentine—what they called dipping turpentine.

We had the barrel sitting on a platform on top of a 4X4, a wagon without wheels, pulled by a mule. We went through the woods from one turpentine tree to another collecting the metal containers, just like gathering eggs from a henhouse.

There were hundreds of them out there.

Later on, we started traveling up near a town called Bunnell to pick potatoes. We'd follow the plow, pick them up, and put them in a sack.

That was very good because they allowed us to take home plenty of white potatoes. We had potato salad, mashed potatoes, baked potatoes, potatoes chopped up in stew beef, all kinds of potatoes.

It reminded me of when we picked cotton back out on the plantation in Cordele, but anyway, after we bagged the potatoes and made sure we put our name on the sack, we stacked them in the middle of the row in the potato field. All our bags were recorded then they were collected and driven to a grader in Bunnell.

Nine

Caddying

One day when I was thirteen, sitting in the classroom at the Rigby School, the principal came in and said the Oceanside Country Club was looking for some boys to be caddies for the SALLY (South Atlantic Women's Amateur Championship), which was played at what is now the Oceanside Country Club in Ormond Beach.

"Would any of you be interested in earning sixty-five cents for the day?

I raised my hand.

"James? You would like to caddy?"

"Yes, ma'am, but I don't know anything about golf. What does a caddy do?"

"You're a big, strong, boy, and you can count, so you'll do fine. You carry the golfer's bag and when she asks you for a number three club, you hand it to her. "

"That's it?"

"That's it."

We had to dress in uniforms. We wore caps to match our sweaters. Our outfits were orange and black with our number on the front and our name on the back. We carried the bags because there were no carts at that time.

The lady I was caddying for would ask for a specific club and I'd present it. When she'd hit the ball, I'd have to watch and follow. Then I'd stand near the ball until she arrived to hit it again. If the ball went too far into the woods, I would look in from the course to see if I could find it, but I didn't have to enter if I didn't find it easily because there were a lot of rattlesnakes in those woods. We also had to wash dirty balls at one of the ball washing stations along the golf course.

If one caddy worked for two ladies at the same time, the caddy could carry one bag on each shoulder. The bags weren't that heavy because they didn't have a whole lot of clubs. We all wanted that opportunity because caddying for two would earn us a dollar instead of sixty-five cents. This was big money.

Beach Pavillion Clubhouse at the Golf Course, Ormond Beach, FL

The women did not think of us as male human beings. They called all of us Boy even though our names were clearly printed on our sweaters. When they played in hot weather and they became uncomfortable, they had no problem stepping into the bushes and taking off their underwear. They gave it to us to put in their bags. This was a common thing to do because they did not consider us men.

I caddied for such people as Patty Berg, Betty Hicks, and Babe Didrikson Zaharias at the SALLY.

As for working with the men, they had heavier and bigger bags, so they would pay us a little bit more. They also called us Boy, but working for them wasn't quite so humiliating.

Later we had a chance to make money by caddying at the Riviera Country Club and that was a good experience. We had the same type of clientele, but for some reason they paid more than the ones at the Oceanside Country Club. Riviera didn't have the uniforms like the Oceanside had.

Ten

More Hotel Work

When I wasn't caddying, I worked in the kitchens at the Ormond Hotel. I started out washing pots and doing food prep for the cooks, including peeling potatoes and carrots.

After a while I got promoted to bellhop and elevator operator.

One of the most fascinating things I encountered was the water-operated elevator at the Ormond Hotel. It had two big old tanks on top of the roof with a rope and a valve on each tank. Inside the elevator car, I'd pull on one of the ropes, which caused the water to flow into to the other tank so the elevator went up. Pulling the other rope returned the water to the first tank, and made the elevator went down. Oftentimes the elevator would stop as much as ten inches off the floor. I had to keep wriggling the ropes from left to right until they matched up. It took a lot of skill. The first couple of weeks I worked on it, "Watch your step," was my mantra.

We never got any tips during the week when we were doing this, but we had our nameplate on our uniform and on Saturday morning at ten o'clock all the staff would come down to the lobby and get in line. That included all the servants, chambermaids, elevator operators, bellhops, door men, everyone who provided some type of service to the guests. The hotel provided the guests with little brown envelopes with our names on them. Guests tipped us right then according to the service we provided. They put whatever amounts they wanted in the envelopes—sometimes they'd give a quarter or fifty cents—then they paraded along the line searching for the name badge to match the envelope. We had some big shots that came and for party of four we might earn a dollar. We called them a "live-wire." "I got a live-wire tonight." I didn't see too many of those, but I always hoped.

The more envelopes we got, the more it showed we were giving a lot of service and we received commendations from the manager. A few guys didn't get many envelopes, but I made myself available for service and did pretty well.

There were fourteen rocking chairs on the verandah of the Hotel. Every morning before we could let anybody sit on them, we had to wipe them down and dry them because they'd been sitting out in the open and got damp. We always had to do it in a hurry before any of the guests arrived. That was one of the things I disliked about working at the hotel, but they fed us good.

The hotel had its own power plant and water plant, and all the hotels had segregated living quarters for their help who wanted to stay there, especially those working the night shift. Ours was in this long building in the back. The white help lived on one side and the black help on the other. And of course we had different pay scales. The hotel also had an employee dining room where they fed us.

Some of the help who worked in the hotel laundry stayed there in the living quarters. Some of my friends and relatives worked in the laundry with white employees folding linen, and some of them worked the presser doing the same job. I heard one of the white guys kid the others about how much money he earned, but there was nothing we could do about it. For myself, I was glad to have a job. That was just one of the discrepancies that existed at that time.

After we had served breakfast and finished cleaning up the dining room we had nothing to do for an hour or two so we could go to the living quarters and take a break. The headwaiter always insisted we change and put on fresh uniforms before each meal. After serving lunch about two o'clock we didn't have to come back until four, so we had another couple of hours to rest and change.

P1416   Florida Special at Ormond Hotel, Ormond Beach, Fla.

One time, a tour bus arrived, and the guests had all their luggage tagged with numbers. Every person had two pieces with the same number on it. When they came in we unloaded the luggage and lined it up across the lobby so we could sort it all together. It was a simple and easy way of keeping track.

I had my clipboard with the numbers on it in order. When the guests registered and gave us their names I wrote them against the numbers. As the bell captain, I then had the other bellhops pull their luggage out and put their names on it.

One particular guy from South Carolina came up and watched me. I held my clipboard and told the others what to do. He followed me around looking at me real strange. After a while he said, "What's your name, boy?"

"James," I said.

"He can read. He can read," he said to another traveler.

"Oh yes. They can read," the other guy replied.

"They can read down here?" another man asked. "Son of a gun."

I thought it unusual that they found it difficult to believe I could read simply because I was a black male. I guess I wasn't supposed to be able to read.

I also worked at the Coquina Hotel, which was different from the Ormond Hotel, but no better, no worse. During the summer all the hotels on the beach closed because it was hot and none of them were air conditioned. A few had fans, and the ones on the ocean side got a little breeze, but once it got real hot in the summer, they all closed up.

I was bell-hopping there. My job was to help check in the guests. One day the manager told us in a firm voice so we knew he wasn't fooling around, "When you go up to check those guests in, don't look at the women on the beach, those white women, if you want a job. Don't look out there."

I pretty much obeyed. Well, ninety percent of the time anyway. If somebody called in and said they wanted an oceanfront room, I'd be given a key and told, "Go up there and open the window so the room will cool off and check to see if everything is all right in the room." So I'd go up to the room and open the shades. The first time I looked down at the beach the only thing I saw was a lot of old white women with one piece bathing suits. I didn't see anything they needed to hide or keep me from seeing. That was kind of disappointing. Anyway, it didn't bother me to take a peep out there once in a while because nothing was exciting. But that was the law. That was their rule and we had to adhere to it.

That brings to mind a story my father told me about a man named Dempsey who worked on that Georgia plantation. Dempsey, under orders from the plantation owner, was chopping wood at the big house. The lady of the house was sitting out on the porch, watching him. She made a reference to Dempsey's strength, telling her husband, "Oh boy, if you could do that." That made her husband real mad.

"What are you doing looking at him?" he asked, then he went out to the yard and told Dempsey to cut wood out on the other side of the house, saying, "Don't cut wood in sight of the ladies. They shouldn't be seeing you from the porch. Go right 'round to the other side of the barn and do your chopping."

One thing we didn't ever do was to make eye contact with a white woman. This was strictly against the rules. If she called to tell us to do something, we could not get closer than about ten feet. When she spoke to us, we had to hold our heads down and look the other way, "Yes ma'am, Yes ma'am." If we looked up, or if she said one of us looked at her, we really were in big trouble. So when that lady made reference to the fact that Dempsey had an attractive body, this really upset the husband, though she never said he looked at her. After the owner sent him to go chop the wood in a different location, he still wasn't satisfied. He followed Dempsey to the barn and told him, "Get back to the field and don't ever show yourself around here chopping wood again."

The husband, still unhappy about his wife's remarks, decided he had to get rid of the man. He couldn't have his wife saying nice things about a black worker. "I don't need him on my farm anymore."

He dismissed Dempsey the next day. "You have one hour to leave or you won't be able to leave here alive." That was all he had to say.

Dempsey took off through the woods to the railroad track. He grabbed on to a little red train. When it started going up those hills it slowed down to almost a snail's pace, so it was easy for him to jump on it. That was the end of him, until he sent for his family to come live up north. He told them how he got a better job, could save a little money, and so they joined him.

This happened to families on a regular basis; one of the members would go out of state, usually up north. Once they got situated, they sent for their family.

The exodus from the south evolved because of the way people were being treated on the farms. They received letters from others who had already left, telling them how good their lives were and what good times they were having. The word got around and the best and brightest workers, the strong young men and women, began leaving the farm. Then they too, wrote letters, so the exodus continued.

The people were in debt and all. I guess we were a part of that crowd too, because we also got out of there.

I think that from the stage where I was a little black boy on the plantation to where I am right now I consider the metamorphosis. I think that is the best way to describe my situation. We were all in a state where we just were—we were happy until we found out something different.

In my early teens I got a job as a page at the Riviera Hotel, a grand establishment. Today it's an assisted living facility on U. S. 1. My chores were to walk around the lobby whenever there was a message for a guest. I'd have to shout out loudly and clearly, "Paging Mr. So and So, Paging Mr. So and So." I'd walk all through the lobby, the dining room, all the public rooms and then outdoors on the grounds. While dressed in my uniform, I also had a tray full of cigars and cigarettes for sale. It had a leather strap to hang it around my neck. That's one good job that went by the wayside over the years, what with intercoms and now cell phones. Add to that all the no smoking bans in public establishments.

One of the benefits that aided the metamorphosis of this black boy was my experience with a lot of formal behavior because I worked in facilities that housed the well-to-do. I was exposed to people with real money. Unlike at the plantation, my employers had no qualms about us working in and around white people. I learned table manners and proper social behavior by observing the men and women, who mostly didn't even notice me.

Eleven

The War Years

I always had something to do. During the lean times of the war years, we got out our shoeshine boxes, went down to the hotels where the female army women of the Women's Army Corp (we all called the women WACs) lived when they came here for training. They took over all the hotels and motels. We'd sit out front on the sidewalk waiting for them to come out. We shined their shoes and asked for ten cents, but most of them gave me fifteen. I really cleaned up because they all had to have clean shoes, so coming and going, they'd stop by and get a quick polish. They kept me and the other shoeshine boys busy.

There were lots of jobs especially for young boys and women because most of the young men had been drafted and sent off to war. We had a real good economy going for us during those years.

During wartime, we couldn't have lights that enemies could see from the ocean at night. All cars driving along the beach at night had to have the top half of the headlights painted so just enough light shone through the bottom to see to drive. I helped tape over the lights on the cars. No lights were allowed in the houses or on the streets near the beach either, not even street lights. If there were, they were painted.

My dad was one of the air raid wardens for our block. Like all the wardens, he wore a little band on his arm that said CD for Civil Defense. Armed with a stick, they patrolled from one end of the block to the other.

We had air raid drills. The sirens were the signal for everybody to rush inside, lock the doors, and turn off all the lights. The practice would last about an hour. When the all clear signal sounded we could turn the lights back on and open the windows.

Some people kept their lights on and just pulled the shades down. If my father saw any crack of light he knocked on the door and warned them if they didn't turn their lights off they would be subject to arrest. The rules were strict. Fortunately, most people respected the law and followed his instructions with no problems.

I was proud of my father when he became an Air Raid Warden. Here's the pamphlet that told his job.

Your Duties as Air Raid Warden.

You have been chosen as Air Raid Warden of your Sector because you are known to be reliable and responsible and because you have the needed qualities to lead, direct, and help the people entrusted to your care. In your Sector are the homes of some hundreds of your friends and neighbors. It will be your responsibility to

67

see that everything possible is done to protect and safeguard those homes and citizens from the new hazards created by attack from the air or by enemies from within our gates. As an Air Raid Warden you have specific duties to perform. You must study them, review them, practice them over and over so that you may carry them out in an air raid without failure or error. You must know your Sector as intimately as others know their own homes. You must know your people well. To them, you are the embodiment of all Civilian Defense. In every way, you must seek to gain their confidence so that in any time of stress you may more easily calm and reassure them and avert panic. As you become better acquainted with the individuals in your Sector, you will learn whom to call upon for informal help at such times. You are not a policeman nor a fireman nor a doctor, although your duties are related to theirs. As an Air Raid Warden, you have a unique position in American community life. It is a position of leadership and trust that demands an effort not less than your best.

Duties Preliminary to Air Attack*
The Senior Warden of each Sector is responsible for seeing that all Wardens in his Sector receive this course.

- First Aid. —A 10-hour practical course con- ducted by the American Red Cross.

- B. Methods of Combating Incendiary Bombs. —Lectures and drill as arranged by local Fire Departments under men who have received special training for instructors at the Civilian Defense Schools. Texts will consist of material furnished at Civilian Defense Schools and publications issued or recommended by the Office of Civilian Defense.
- C. Protection Against Gas. —Lectures con- ducted by specially trained instructors or Reserve Officers. Texts will consist of material furnished at Civilian Defense Schools and publications issued or recommended by the Office of Civilian Defense. D. Reports. —A special course in making out, forwarding, and recording reports, arranged by the Chief Warden.

Detailed Knowledge of the Sector. Under direction of the Senior Warden, a large scale map will be constructed and hung on the wall of the Post to show location of:

- All buildings, the character of each, and access doors to streets and alleys. Also indicate coal chutes, freight delivery entrances, and in cities, power, steam, or telephone tunnels for use in event of building collapse. (In black.)

- B. Fire hydrants, alarm boxes, auxiliary water storage, special fire-fighting equipment, fire stations. (In brown.)
- C. Places of special danger, such as oil-storage tanks, filling stations, lumber yards, other highly inflammable materials, firetrap houses, weak walls. (In red.)
- D. Emergency places of refuge such as deep, well-protected vaults or cellars, safe inside rooms. (In blue.)
- E. Police stations, first-aid posts, hospitals, decontamination stations, road repair stores, and other organized services of Civilian Defense. (By suitable symbol.) It is not enough to assemble this information on a map. As an Air Raid Warden, you must know it by heart, and be able to find any required position or place in a complete blackout.
- Detailed Knowledge of the People. The people themselves must be studied carefully as to temperament and ability to assist in emergency. The aged and infirm and all children under 5 years of age should be listed and arrangements made to provide them with help if necessary. All persons with special training useful in Civilian Defense should be registered. All of this information should be recorded in a bound book kept at the Post which will

list the following specifically: Doctors
(give specialty). Nurses (graduate or
practical). Drugstores (nearest, if none
in Sector).

A handbook for air raid wardens

We saw big ships patrolling far out in the ocean.
Some people said they were German. If a ship sank out
there, we never knew whose it was. The smoke
lingered for hours. We heard of German submarines
coming close to shore, but I never saw one.

Sometimes officials stopped the traffic on the
bridge to the beach side. There were certain times
when we were not allowed to cross or guards in certain
sections checked everybody before crossing. So
security was pretty tight. It was exciting. It taught us to
be alert in case of war in America. It was said the
German ships could come in close enough to fire on
land if they needed or wanted to, although we had
American ships patrolling: destroyers, torpedo boats
and submarines.

***

Franklin D. Roosevelt created a program
originally called The Works Progress Administration
and renamed in 1939 as The Work Projects
Administration, WPA for short. This was part of his
"American New Deal." The program employed
millions of unemployed people (mostly unskilled men)
to carry out public works projects, including the
construction of public buildings and roads. During that
same period a big coquina bed, or shell pit, was

opened in National Garden, a little town just north of Ormond off US 1. It provided work for a lot of people. The coquina rock was used for the large buildings still standing today, the band-shell, walls and clock tower on the boardwalk, the armory and other buildings. There was a lot to do around Daytona and Ormond Beach. The WPA workers put those buildings up with the rock my father and others delivered.

There was a lot of good going on and, of course a little bad, too, though we couldn't have a whole lot of bad stuff because our jailhouse had only one cell. Most of the time it was empty. When there was someone in there, mostly it was someone who got drunk and wanted to fight. The police picked him up and let him stay overnight. They had very few murders and very few felons at that time. If somebody got out of hand and shot somebody, the sheriff took him to Deland, the county seat, about forty five minutes west of the beach and locked them up over there. We couldn't house them in Ormond.

***

Another interesting thing that happened in the 40's in Daytona Beach was that the former dictator of Cuba, Fulgencio Batista bought a home here, and even though he was mulatto, he lived on the beachside of Daytona Beach, in a riverfront home about ten houses north of the Main Street Bridge. We went down around Dunn Lumber Company on the railroad track and tried to see him. He came in with a huge entourage and security, greeted and protected by our entire police department, sheriff's department, FBI, and civil service. It was more activity than when the president came to town. They blocked off the whole train station. They unloaded tons of large boxes and put them in trucks and vans and took them over to his house on Halifax.

***

One evening Dad came home and announced we were taking a trip to Georgia. "We can get some watermelon and corn and stuff and bring it back down to Florida and sell it."

"Can I drive the truck? I can reach the pedals now so you won't even have to fix it up for me," I said. My brothers laughed, but they had been too little to remember when I drove the watermelon truck up in Cordele when I'd been eight years old. I drove a truck while the men in my family tossed watermelons into the back to take to the farmers' market in town. Dad used cushions to raise me up so I could see over the dashboard. My feet didn't reach the pedals, so he put the truck in low gear and told me to keep the steering wheel steady along the row. The truck moved slowly enough so they could pick and toss the melons. When we reached the end of a row, Dad hopped up, took over to turn the truck around, and we'd go down along the next row.

On one of the trips to Georgia, the truck's fuel pump gave out on us in a remote rural section. We had to push it about three or four miles to a combination gas station, garage, and little restaurant. The mechanic said the fuel pump was gone, so he sent somebody into town to get another one. That was about nine o'clock in the morning. We had no choice except to hang around there. He worked a while, took a coffee break with some of his buddies, then came back and worked a little more.

"If I took so many breaks like that at the golf club, I wouldn't have a job for five minutes," I said.

Dad told me, "We're at his mercy, son. Let's don't say anything to annoy him. Be patient. He'll get it done."

Around noon, white men began entering the restaurant. The food smelled good and we were hungry, so my father asked the man there, "Can my boys get something to eat out of the place?"

"Sure. Go on around to the back," he said, and told his wife, "Let them boys have some meat back there."

We crowded around the back door to the kitchen and she asked, "Whatcha want?"

"Whatcha got?"

She named two or three things, sandwiches and all. The others ordered sandwiches.

"I'd like the stew beef and rice," I said. That sounded pretty good to me.

She came back with wrapped sandwiches and handed them over. She had a brown paper bag with my stew beef and rice in it. She had placed two slices of bread in the bottom of the bag and the stew beef and rice on top of that. As she handed me the bag, she told me to hold the bottom. I took it and asked if she had a fork or spoon I could eat it with. She told me to go sit on a log and drink it. "That's what the others do," she said.

We went back to the truck. I tried to eat some of it, as much as I could, but it was hot and running over everything. I lost half of it and ate whatever I could salvage out of the bag. It was a pretty messy operation.

Even today, I say that was pretty mean the way we were served and treated. And we had to pay for it. Daddy had given us money to buy what we wanted. I avoided the restaurant the rest of the day.

Our big truck had an enclosed body, with our blankets and things in the back. If we wanted to go to the bathroom, we had to use a big can we kept in the back of the truck since we weren't allowed to use the facilities at the gas station.

The repair job was finally finished around five o'clock so we finally continued out trip up to Cordele. When we arrived, we went to the farmers' market. We loaded up with watermelons and cantaloupe and came on back to Ormond Beach, where we peddled them on the streets. We bought the watermelons in Georgia for fifteen or twenty cents apiece, with some big ones for a quarter. Cantaloupe were ten and fifteen cents. We sold them for three times that much when we got back to Florida. We did pretty well.

***

There were other problems traveling in the south in those days.

One time, my brothers, a couple of other family members and I were traveling back from a funeral in Georgia when the gas gauge showed we were almost empty. We stopped at a gas station in a small town in Florida. Even though driving a fairly nice car, we were refused service. So we went down the road a ways and one of my brothers, the most untidily dressed one, took the can they always carried in the car and walked back to the service station. The same guy who'd refused earlier sold him a can full of gas.

On another occasion, on a Monday morning, coming back from another funeral in Georgia, we stopped at a service station. We were wearing shirts and ties, although we didn't have our jackets on. We knew wearing a shirt and tie, or being nicely dressed, would be resented, especially on a weekday when everybody was expected to be working. A man came out, but before he sold us any gas, asked us a thousand questions.

"What you all doing dressed up? You all preachers?"

We told him about the funeral and where we were going, so he finally sold us some gas. He wouldn't check our oil. One of my brothers wanted to check the oil. Another said we'd better not raise our hood to check it at his service station. So, we went on down the road before we checked it.

That's just the way it was in those days. It was stupid, but it's a fact. That's the way it happened.

My dad used that big old truck to haul fill dirt, peat moss, all kinds of shrubbery and even palm trees. We did a lot of work over on the beachside where all those motels were being built. After the seawall was built, it needed to be filled in. This took a lot of fill dirt, and of course, all the black guys in the area that had any kind of truck were paid to haul fill dirt and help get it fixed up so they could landscape it.

At one particular big old motel there were two or three black guys that were doing all of the hauling. They were paid by the load, so they raced to see who could haul the most loads and make the most money. Then a funny thing happened to my dad. Another guy was really hustling and he saw my dad out at the pit getting dirt and he told him he had just left the hotel, and that the owner told him to hold up for a couple of days. However, this was not true. We held up, did something else, and didn't haul any dirt over there for a couple of days.

Then my dad decided he would go over there and check to find out when they were going to need us to start back hauling dirt. So this guy, the owner, came out walking real fast to our truck, real fast, and he said, "Frank!"

Dad answered.

"I thought you were dead," the owner said.

"What do you mean, you thought I was dead?"

"Yeah, the other guy told me you died in an accident, and your friends were covering for you. He said he knew you real well, so we gave him a card to send to your family. It had twenty-five dollars in it for your wife and kids because you and your boys did such a good job."

He told my dad that he was his favorite delivery man because he dumped the dirt and spread it right where the owner wanted it.

"I don't know why he would tell me you were dead except so he could haul this stuff in here and make the money, but he won't be able to work here anymore. "

And so my dad said, "Well, you certainly won't see him again if I see him first."

He was going to contact him, but said there wouldn't be any violence.

Anyway, my dad finally caught up with this guy. The guy said he'd been having a real hard time and he needed to make some extra money. He ended up giving Dad the condolence card, and the twenty-five dollars.

At that time people were doing all kinds of things to make a few dollars. Lots of dishonesty popped up. It was just as bad when they were building all those buildings out of coquina rock under the WPA. They hired workers by the day and the first one there would say everybody else was sick.

I thought that was kind of a unique trick this guy pulled on my father, but it didn't work for long. As a result of his trickery, he was fired from the job and my dad stayed around for a long time and continued to do business.

***

One thing I had a lot of fun doing was selling mullet. A canal ran alongside U. S. 1 right into the Tomoka River. My brother Jerry and I dug our own bait and went up there to catch mullet. As fast as we threw our hook in, we'd pull one out. I had a little red wagon, which we filled with fish. We didn't have any ice to keep them cold so we put water in there so the fish would kind of keep cool. I put a cloth over them. When we had filled the wagon, we'd take the fish into town and go up and down each street selling them for five cents each. People would buy three or four. Some days we would make a couple of trips to the canal.

At one time, I had a job babysitting horses near the Sterthaus Dairy Farm. A man pulling a horse trailer behind his truck brought six or eight horses and left them in the pasture for four or five days. I had to go out there and watch the horses all day. He came back every evening.

I could sit out there and play, or do whatever I wanted to, just as long as I watched the horses. I could even get on my bicycle and go home if I needed to because I didn't live too far from the pasture. I was just supposed to make sure they didn't escape through the fence, and make sure no one took them. I didn't have to feed or water them. The man had a big shed there with plenty of water in the trough and plenty of food. That was one of the best jobs I had during that time because I got paid real good.

I always had a job. After the horses, I used to throw papers for the Jacksonville Journal. It was pretty good money, but I had to be up at 5:30 in the morning to meet the Greyhound bus at the Gulf service station on the corner of Yonge Street and Granada. The driver gave me my papers, I signed a little slip, then delivered them. After that I went home, ate breakfast, and went to school at Rigby.

Another job I had was making brooms in a factory right there on Granada down near the railroad track. It was interesting to see how palmetto bushes were stripped down and the rods made into brooms in the factory. We made all kinds of brooms, not just regular household brooms, but big brooms that were mounted on a machine. They were shipped all over the country.

That job paid quite well. Most anything that paid money was good; we thought so anyway because we were used to working sunup to sundown on the plantation in Georgia without getting anything individually. Broom making was interesting, and I enjoyed it.

I also enjoyed shagging balls on the golf course. I'd go out to the driving range and the golfer would pull out his big bag of balls at the tee, give me the empty bag, and I went way out on the golf course to pick up the balls as he hit them. Once I filled the bag he'd pay me. For one bag I probably made about sixty cents. After two I could wind up with a dollar twenty-five. If he was a big tipper he might give me a dollar and a half.

I preferred to shag for the good golfers, watching how far they could drive the balls. They hit them in a straight line toward me. I was the target who enjoyed seeing them make a good drive. I might even back up to try to encourage them to hit a little harder. I picked up MacGregors and Titleists, filled up the bag and returned it to the golfer. Then, he did it all over again. That was a nice clean job. Some of the men could tip real well.

Twelve

Working Up North

One year, when I worked at the Princess Issena Hotel, since the hotels in Florida closed down for the summer, I had the opportunity to go work at Ft. William Henry on Lake George in New York. I drove up with a friend in an old Buick. Because of the times, we chose to drive straight through, not knowing where we would be allowed to spend the night. As soon as we arrived and were shown our living quarters, I knew things were going to be very different in the north. Our accommodations were first class compared to what we had in Ormond. The hotel guests included folk such as the Vanderbilts and Kennedys.

The hotel was concerned about providing proper service. They were real particular. They wanted the staff to be intelligent. Servers had to be clean and dressed properly, and I remember some of the white women that I worked for would say to some of the black women that were working, "You don't have to say, 'yes ma'am' to me or 'yes ma'am' to the women. We don't demand that, the ma'am part. You can say,

'Yes Miss Sobrisky,' or 'Yes, Mrs. Nova.' Just say yes and state the name."

The men were more particular than the women. They always wanted us to say, "Yes, sir" and "No, sir."

The town people, unused to seeing black people, considered us a novelty and treated us well. We could go into all the shops with no problem. After that summer, I was happy to volunteer to work up north again.

The following year, I worked at the Lamarnier Inn on Lake Waramaug in Connecticut. They had a casino down on the lake in front of the hotel where they had entertainment for the guests. Some of the cream of the crop entertained during the summer months. I met Rita Hayworth, Orson Wells, and Everett Sloan, who were filming a sequel for *Lady from Shanghai* in New York City and came up to the inn on weekends. It was quite an experience to meet these top-notch people in the entertainment industry.

I worked as a waiter in some of the finest places. For me it was a learning and humbling experience to serve the rich and famous; to get close enough to them that they called me by my first name. And when I provided good service, I received great tips.

I also had a chance to work as a bartender that summer. I didn't do a whole lot, but one night Mr. Noah, the manager called me in to his office. "James, do you think you could tend bar this afternoon and evening?"

Surprised by this request, because Frank, the regular bartender was white, I said, "I could, yes, sir."

"Frank called in sick and you're the only employee available with some experience mixing drinks."

I didn't have a whole lot of experience, but I wouldn't turn down an opportunity like this. "I'll be happy to help."

One of my first customers was a young couple. The young man strutted like a peacock, trying to impress his girlfriend. They approached the bar, and he said, "Where's my bartender? Where's Frank?"

"He had an emergency he couldn't come in today," I said. "I'm filling in for him."

He stuck his nose in the air. "Well, I don't want you putting your black hands on my drink."

I replied, "Okay, sir. I'll put on some gloves." I found a pair of rubber gloves and put them on before I served him.

I could see his girlfriend was a little bit put out with the way he was trying to play me down and embarrass me, so I fixed him a real good stiff drink. He had that drink and they sat there and talked. I served them some snacks. He ordered a second drink. Now he was feeling pretty good. They sat and continued drinking and he started feeling real good.

When he was ready for his third drink he said, "Mr. Bartender, give me another drink, sir."

That was quite a change. By that time I had taken off my gloves and he didn't even notice. He continued calling me Mr. Bartender. This fellow changed from being unable to tolerate my black hands to showing respect during the course of the afternoon. I thought that was comical. I think about how a drink can sometimes bring out the niceness in us. But it can also do the reverse, because I had a couple of situations where customers got real mean when they had a few drinks.

***

The summer before I started college, I had a job with the Pepsi Cola Bottling Company.

My father had given me some sound advice. "When you go for a job, even if it's for a ditch digger or trash collector, you never dress for the job. You dress as nicely and neatly as you can. You try to dress like the person who is going to hire you. Look clean, nice. The more you impress them, the better job you'll get. "

That's as true today as it was in 1940.

I went to the Pepsi Cola plant on Ballough Road to apply for a job, wearing nice slacks, shirt, and tie. I was asked what all I could do and I named a few things I had done and explained about my schooling.

The interviewer invited me into the office and told me to sit there for a few minutes.

So I sat down. He went out back and talked with some of the other people in the office. When he returned he asked me, "Are you pretty good in math?"

"Yes, I think so," I said.

"We're going to give you a job in the office."

I felt my face light up with happiness at the prospect of a real office job. I said, "Oh, gee. Good. Thank you!"

He showed me to a little desk right over in the corner, directly in front of the window, where I could look out into the plant and watch all the trucks as they were being loaded and unloaded. He told me he wanted me to be a checker. "I want you to see how many crates they load onto each of the trucks. I want you to count them, so many orange, so many grape, so many regular Pepsis."

It was an easy matter checking them because the secretary gave me a clipboard to hold the checking sheets. They were captioned across the top with Grape Soda, Orange Soda, and all of the different kinds of sodas that they sold. The only thing I had to do was count the number of crates they loaded onto the trucks and write down the number of each drink. That was an easy job. I was now a counter.

At the end of one week the manager said he might have a permanent job for me. That sounded good to me.

He told me, "For one week I had someone checking behind you. We've been checking the checker. And you have been right on the money. You did a good job. We're going to give you a raise and give you your own permanent position."

I nodded politely and thanked him when what I really wanted to do was jump up and shout, "Hooray!"

I stayed there until I was ready to go off to school and they were nice to me when I left.

Thirteen

Florida A&M

I started college in the fall of 1950. For the first two years, I majored in speech and drama. In my junior year, I switched to political science.

I shared a room with my high school friend from Daytona, Willie Fields. We each paid six dollars a month for the room.

During those years I worked at the Duval Hotel in Tallahassee. One morning I was standing by the newspaper rack on the sidewalk and a couple, guests in the hotel, came out with their two little kids. The lady's mother was with them.

There were a couple of steps outside the front door and as they walked out, the mother stumbled. I just happened to be in the right position to catch her so she wouldn't fall and smash her head on the sidewalk. I jumped in front of her, and she landed right in my arms. Once she straightened up and discovered that I was a black bellhop, she said, "Take your black hands off me."

Her daughter said, "Mother, this guy kept you from falling and smashing your head on the sidewalk and you're talking to him like that? You should be ashamed. " She turned to me. "I apologize for the way my mother talked to you. She should have been grateful to you for this."

She then told her husband to give me a tip. He gave me a twenty-dollar bill. When I told the other bellhops what had happened, one of them said, "If I see them coming out again I'm gonna jump in front of her. She can call me whatever she wants so long as that son-in-law takes care of it. Sticks and stones will break my bones, but words will never hurt. " That was a good philosophy that I always lived by.

Nothing exciting or memorable happened while in college, with one exception. I met Carrie McGhee who was studying library science, and we married.

Fourteen

Florida School for Boys in Marianna, Florida

Shortly before graduation, a friend of a friend told me of a job opening with good state benefits, which also provided room and board and free laundry service. That sounded good to me. I went for the interview and got my first job out of college as a counselor with the Florida Industrial School for Boys, later known as the Florida School for Boys, and even later known as the Arthur G. Dozier School for Boys.

This school was for delinquent boys from ages roughly eight until about sixteen. The boys came from all sixty-seven counties in Florida, referred for crimes from simple truancy, shoplifting, being drunk or unruly in school, to murder. Though they were sent to the school to be reformed, I quickly learned the system was not set up to rehabilitate them.

I drove down the narrow dirt road that led up to the camp on a hot summer day in 1954. The left side of the road could have been a scene from my youth in Cordele. Black boys were hoeing and digging the farm crops that supplied food for the school. On the right side, white boys lingered around pens and cages filled with chickens and rabbits. Two white boys with long sticks herded cows into a barn. Clearly the division of labor had the black boys doing the heavy work, while the white ones worked at the less strenuous jobs.

The boys were housed in "cottages," each with upstairs living quarters for a counselor. It was a full-sized apartment, with a kitchenette. The boys' dormitory, bathrooms, and showers were downstairs. At the end of the building, a recreation room held a ping-pong table, and tables where they could sit and play checkers and other games. Each cottage also had its own little basketball court to provide some outdoor activity.

At night the boys' working clothes were locked up. They were issued a gown to sleep in and were allowed to keep their underwear. The reasoning being that without any clothes, there was less possibility of them running away.

There was no air conditioning in the building. Upstairs, in the counselors' apartments, we had electric fans, including in the windows, but downstairs the boys had none, and hoped for a little breeze to enter through the windows. Thus, their windows were always open, and they could just jump out the window if they wanted. They were not locked up as such. Their quarters depended on what age bracket or what grade they were in. They got merits or demerits according to whether they were good or got into trouble.

The division of labor matched the inmate population as well. Black men supervised the black boys; white men oversaw the white boys. I soon learned our housing was equally divided.

Several cottages housed boys separated, not only by race, but also according to their ages. I was in charge of a bunch of cottages holding about 35 or 40 boys at a time. The population revolved with some leaving as others arrived.

When the boys first arrived, they were classified as Rookies. At the end of thirty days, if they showed any progress, they would move up to Explorer, and later, Pioneer. The top rank was Ace. The authorities meted out grades periodically to show their progress. The only thing they really taught the boys was to adhere to a schedule. They went to bed at a certain time, got up at a certain time, ate at a certain time, and had to be on the job at a certain time. That was pretty much the extent of their rehabilitation process.

The boys' duty was to farm the school land, a large area located five miles from any town, surrounded by swamps and woods. Everything we ate was grown on the farm, vegetables, corn and potatoes, all kinds of cabbage, different types of greens. They also raised cows, hogs, goats, rabbits and chickens.

The worst place for boys to be was in a group called The Grubs. Grubs had to get up at four o'clock in the morning to milk the cows and feed the animals.

There was one road in and out. No one left without permission, and that also included the staff. We had to sign in and out. They were very strict with the staff. If we wanted to leave for the weekend or any appointment, we had to put in leave slips.

As far as the boys were concerned, their "rehabilitation" was to do their job, and work properly.

They had a dress code—for example, pants couldn't touch the ground. If they didn't dress accordingly, they would get a demerit.

On the bright side, we had the best food to be found anywhere. Besides raising all our own vegetables and meat, the boys worked in the butcher shop. Adults were hired to slaughter the livestock and do all the other things that were necessary for processing the food. The food was excellent and it was all free.

When officials visited to inspect the school, they were always given nice package to take back, steaks, chops, and other cuts of meat.

Despite the intention of the school, and the fact that the boys were delinquents, I found the discipline methods horrifying. If a boy broke a rule, any rule, he was punished severely.

There was a little cement block building, dubbed the Ice Cream Factory, also called The White House, about eight by ten feet, furnished with a cot and a chair. It had one door, and one small window near the ceiling, which allowed in a little light. A boy sent there for punishment would have to take off all his clothes and lay on the cot, face down, holding onto each side to receive three whacks.

If the boy twisted or moved after the first hit, the guard started over again until he hit him three times in a row without his moving. Sometimes they just beat the feeling out of them. The boys came out bruised and bloody.

The last straw for me was when they called me in one night to show me a particular boy who had just been "punished." His skin was broken and he was in the shower trying to clean up. Water got in behind his broken skin and he had a big water bubble. It continued to bleed. We didn't have a first aid kit or anything to fix him up with, but I got a big wad of Vaseline and ripped up a sheet and tied strips tightly around his wounds to stop the bleeding. I gave him three or four aspirins. He was devastated, shaking so badly, I could hardly wrap him. That was just ugly.

A few of the boys were pretty smart. They hid clothes behind the bushes during the day and at night they would hop out of the window to escape. Sadly, that was a mistake for most of them. The word would soon get out that someone had hit the bushes and a posse would be formed to search for them. Sometimes they would be brought back—sometimes we didn't hear from them ever again.

If they were caught, they received a good whipping and were then kept them in confinement for a while before being put into the Grubbs category. It was the epitome of cruel and unusual punishment.

Instead of having a place where they could teach, train, and reform them, the goal was to punish them into shape, which didn't work. The smarter boys figured it out quickly enough; they learned to pretend they were little angels to get promoted so they could get out as quickly as possible.

When a boy was released, an official notified the judge of the county where the boy was from that he was being discharged. Usually, a counselor would pick him up and take him directly to his family.

If a boy got away and wasn't caught, or something else happened to him and he went missing, the family and judge from that particular county would be notified. When a boy ran away, the family knew he wasn't coming home, because that was the first place the law would look for him. So they said, "Well, he escaped, we'll be hearing from him."

In many cases, weeks, months, even years would pass and they never heard from their child again. This situation eventually threw up a red flag and is what led to an investigation up in Marianna.

I worked there for nearly two years before I said goodbye to that ungodly place. When I first started as a counselor I felt good about the well-paying job, the benefits, and the potential for being able to help those young boys. During my time there, I made every effort within my power to make changes, but my words fell on deaf ears. That place haunts me to this day.

Although I had wondered what happened to the boys who'd gone missing, I never even fathomed that many were murdered and buried right there. Chilling.

In recent years a lot of concern has come about regarding unmarked graves found on the campus. It's open for speculation, but forty-eight were found and an attempt made to identify them through DNA. This is an ongoing investigation.

Fifteen

Carrie and I Working in Florida

A few weeks before I was to marry Carrie, Len Jenkins, called and asked me, "Why are you working over at that place? I can give you a job right here in automobile insurance. All you have to do is take the test then you can make some big bucks. "

Much as I hated to leave the boys, I was relieved to find a less horrific way to make a living. As my wife's family all lived in Tallahassee, and I knew it would make her happy to be near them, I took the test, passed and began a new career. It paid far better than I ever expected, and I didn't have to face those unfortunate boys every day of the week.

When Carrie and I married, The Tallahassee newspaper printed the story: Tallahassee Lassie Marries Ormond Beach Beau.

We honeymooned at a beautiful motel right on the beach, American Beach, west of Jacksonville. Florida wasn't integrated yet, so we had to find a black motel. There were only about four in all of Florida. The motel was really nice.

I worked at the insurance company, doing well, when they decided they wanted to open a branch office on the East Coast between St. Augustine and Melbourne. I spoke up and told them Daytona Beach would be a great place. I sold them on the idea, they accepted it, and I moved back to Daytona.

Carrie was a librarian at a little school in Tallahassee, Florida. As it was near time for the end of the school year, I went on down to Daytona to set up a life for us there. Because I came from Ormond, it was a natural place for me to find a place to live. Carrie stayed with her parents in Tallahassee. At that time we had our first born, Derek. Though school had closed, Carrie worked in the summer program. I wanted her with me in Daytona Beach, so I met with the principal at Campbell Street High School.

I said to him, "If you ever get an opening at your school, my wife is a teacher up in Tallahassee and I want to bring her down here, so I'm looking for a job for her."

He said, "I don't need a teacher, but I'd give my right arm if I could locate a librarian. "

I said, "A librarian?"

He said, "Yeah."

I said, "Well, that's what my wife is, a librarian."

"You can't make this up."

"No. She's a librarian. She's certified. She's a librarian."

He said, "Well, can you get her here tomorrow?"

I said, "I don't know about tomorrow, but I can get her here in a couple of days."

I opened the car insurance agency in Daytona, but it wasn't long before the manager of the life insurance company that had an office upstairs in our building came calling. They lured me with the job of staff manager. With the promise of better prospects, I switched over and that's where I stayed for the next twenty-five years, retired from there and then started my own agency with my partner, Lilly Young. We created Daniels and Young Insurance Agency.

During those years I became involved in other enterprises. At one time I was in real estate. I had about 24 rental houses which fortunately I sold just before the bottom fell out of the housing market. I had a thrift shop. I worked as a chef at one time because I opened up the first rooftop restaurant in Ormond Beach. It was a small place in a motel, but I had very good business there and it went quite well and was profitable. Things were looking better. It was a long ways from the cotton fields of the Sidney Wells Plantation in Cordele, Georgia to a chef on the beachside in Ormond Beach. It had been several steps in the right direction.

Sixteen

1950s and Urban Renewal

In the original mandate for the Daytona Beach Urban Renewal Program, any person who was displaced from the redevelopment area would be provided standard housing. Of course there were not too many standard houses in the immediate area, so residents had the opportunity to move elsewhere into, transitional areas. The plan was to move them out, redevelop the area, and give them first choice to move back to the particular area from which they had been displaced.

Most of the displaced people received either a relocation fee or were paid for whatever house they were living in. With extra money in their pocket they went out and got themselves fixed up really well because they had been paid top dollar for those old shacks. Once in their new home, in a new area, when offered a chance to return, nobody wanted to sign up.

The developers built according to whatever the homeowners wanted. The situation was meant to be that the homeowners took their money, put it in the bank, and then worked with the redevelopers. The developers realigned and replanted the area giving every lot at least 75' frontage. They added sidewalks, paved the streets, included electricity, sewers, and running water. Once they had put in the new infrastructure, the homeowners were supposed to meet with the developer and pick out the lot they were going to build on; not necessarily the exact area they moved out of. Now everything was nice and clean the developers waited for somebody to make inquiries about building for them. In many instances that never happened, so the developer moved on to something else.

Right now several of those lots still stand vacant because the demand was not there and still isn't. Most people didn't want to come back into that part of town. They got a taste of a much better section, which is understandable because before the HUD program came into being in Daytona Beach did not have an open occupancy policy. Once the officials signed off on that, it meant that nobody regardless of race, color, or creed could be denied an opportunity to relocate to any area of the town. They could do so without discrimination.

We did have people who left permanently. A lot of them moved to South Daytona or Ormond, the west side, and even to the beachside.

The program served a double purpose. It not only helped the people who were being displaced, it upgraded the standard of living for people living in blight that they hadn't been able to afford to escape, and it boosted the economy because real estate agents were having a field day. People were relocated to anywhere they wanted to go, even to the "white" areas that they could not have lived in prior to that. This was one of the greatest things that happened to the blacks in Daytona Beach. Business boomed. Construction business was going good. Developing the infrastructure provided a lot of jobs. Those who had a house got cash money at a good price. With money in hand they were ready to do business. The realtors knew that and hauled people around, showing them houses. This was a considerable achievement for the City and people of Daytona. It was received happily by most. There were only a few opposed to the program. I considered it a blessing—a win-win situation for everybody.

Seventeen

James F. Daniels – Movie Star

During the fifties, I worked in a few films—
films I'm proud to have been involved with. The first
film I worked with was *Gap in the Hedges,* about a
segregated community in Ormond. This was sponsored
and filmed by a production crew from Daytona Junior
College.

Race relations, especially with the police
department, were bad. In this film we were able to
achieve some of the things the movie talked about. I
played the part of an old citizen who was trying to
keep the peace. One white policeman, who was also a
peacemaker, asked to be assigned to the black
community. In the story he became a good friend to
some of the young people which didn't set too well
with some of the other people.

Some citizens wanted to build a fence in the
fictional city with the intention to separate the races.
We did all we could to keep them from building it, but
the radicals outvoted us and they finally built it. We
didn't like the fence, but we couldn't do anything

about having it removed so we protested. And our protest was to plant hedges alongside the fence, effectively hiding it. We left a gap in the hedge to symbolically show that we were not completely segregated.

During the filming we worked with police officers from the local police department who acted in the film. We created fictional incidents where the police were called out. Their crowd control consisted of taking sides with the white folk. But that one white officer who had been working in the black community and knew the people, took a different stance. He knew our little black kids. He knew everybody in the black community. As a result of his having worked in that section of town the black people were better represented. Both the man as an actor and as an officer in real life took some of the young people riding with him in his police vehicle. The filming of this story in this location helped create better relations.

The school showed the film in the area, hoping it would catch on and be shown in other cities in the south.

I was also in a little film I did at Bethune Cookman College dealing with the Mary McLeod Bethune Boulevard. The point was to talk about the businesses located on the main strip of the black community before integration, and what happened to them after we had the urban renewal program. I think I pretty much covered that because as I said, most of those businesses there were operating on a shoestring—marginal profit businesses—once the agency came in and relocated them, and in many instances paid them a nice price for their properties and for their businesses, they pretty much took the money and ran. They didn't want to reestablish their businesses in the other places although we had relocation facilities for them to go. It was a wise thing because after integration the average person found other places to do business.

The biggest movie I was involved in was *Beach Racing, 1903-1958*in 2012, filmed by Daytona State College, with Scott Auerbach as director. It was about racing on the beaches of Ormond, Daytona, and Ponce

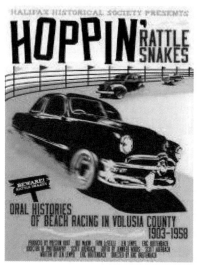

Inlet, the true birthplace of speed and racing. This eventually evolved into the International Speedway which Bill France opened in 1958.

In the film I had a chance to talk about a few of the things I remembered. I talked about Wendell Scott, the first black race driver on the NASCAR circuit. I knew him and his crew because they ate my chicken boxes. I had a restaurant, Chicken, Shrimp, and Fish. I specialized in boxes to go and they ordered an awful lot of them. Other race drivers heard about it and they sent people down to pick up my Chicken, Shrimp, and Fish boxes, mostly fried chicken.

We used to have a good time watching the races on the beach. We parked our bicycles on the side of the road and we'd go through the palmetto bushes toward the beach. Frequently we saw rattlesnakes. Many of them stretched out, some coiled. If they were stretched out, we'd hop over them and keep running until we got to the edge of the palmetto bushes where we would hide, peek through them and watch the cars go past. Because of the danger of hopping rattlesnakes in order to see the races, the movie was titled *Hopping Rattlesnakes*.

Eighteen

Racial differences Georgia to Ormond

People in Georgia and Florida were different—
not only economically, but in attitude. Even the white
racists were different. There was no comparison.

There was also a lot of difference between the
whites in Ormond and the whites in Daytona—
Ormond had a more liberal attitude.

In Daytona we couldn't go on the beach side at
night. We had to have a pass, a work permit, to walk
across the river at night. Even with the work permit it
was better not be out too much after ten o'clock or
there could be trouble just from the white street
people. In Ormond we could walk across the bridge
and wouldn't be hassled.

In Daytona, especially across the Main Street
Bridge, there were little beer joints where some of the
locals hung out. I guess that created a difference
because the Daytona locals harassed any black guy
walking late at night. They shouted and picked on
them. The black guys would take off running and some

of the white guys chased them for a bit. The black guys ran back across the bridge to get out of their antagonists' way. That didn't happen in Ormond because our hometown whites had their bars in another section of town, on the other side of the railroad tracks.

Ormond was unique because all of the blacks lived on the east side of the railroad tracks. This was unusual because blacks were on US 1 and all of the whites, upper class rich people, lived right on the river, Riverside Drive, or Oceanside right next to blacks. So we were kind of a buffer between the high class whites and the low class whites who lived across the railroad tracks west of us. We were between what used to be called Cracker Woods and the riverfront, the high class white people and the ocean folk.

We were in a nice location strategically because we didn't have to come in contact with the radical white element. White folk came through our section of town to go to work. We didn't bother them. The whole city, the whole atmosphere in Ormond, was different from Daytona. The poor people, white and black, worked together in the hotels and places that provided for the rich. Daytona was completely different. The blacks lived on the west side of the railroad tracks, and the whites were on the riverfront and Ridgewood Avenue.

In Georgia, plantation owners bragged to the other plantation owners as to who had the best workers. One would say he had the best group of "niggers" working for him and the other would say his group picked more cotton and did more work. We were not a human beings, just little black piglets "niggerlets". That was the class they put us in. Owners

105

bragged about their people, and the others bragged right back, as to who did the most manual labor, and who were less trouble.

The conversations and ideas were different in Ormond Beach. The white people in Ormond Beach, for the most part, bragged about how *smart* their help was. They would see who could out-dress their maids, the chauffeur, and the people that worked around them. They tried to make their help look better and more intelligent than the others.

They dressed their chauffeurs in pretty white shirts, black suits, caps, and well-shined shoes and had them stand out by their cars when they went to different functions. Their chauffeurs brought them down from their homes on the ocean front or around in the area and just stood around.

There would be a line of six or eight cars in front of the Ormond Hotel or Oceanside Country Club wherever they held a function. The drivers opened the car doors so the owners could walk out all feeling like a million dollars.

They had the same attitude with their maids. They dressed them up with aprons and head-piece to work around the house. When guests visited, they had well-presented people to serve them. They also made sure they were well-mannered and taught them how to serve properly, as well as look beautiful.

We were working for completely different people. Having the best cars and the best-looking help were their bragging rights.

Ormond had most of the people from the northern states. These rich people were not too particular about being racially separated. They wanted us to serve them. They took us in and helped us make something of ourselves instead of playing us down. In fact some of the people became so involved with, and were so close to some of the black families, they even put them in their wills. A lot of the servants received financial benefits, along with real-estate, valuables, and jewelry.

Old organized money lived up and down the John Anderson strip. Only one black person owned a home on John Anderson Drive. She had been left the home by a woman for whom she'd worked many years. Her employer hired an attorney before she died and had him set up everything so the employee would be able to handle her new wealth when the time came. She left her most of her money, stocks, and bonds. This was the type of thing going on in Ormond that did not happen in Cordele, Georgia.

There were other things that came out of the Ormond situation.

Because there were a lot of good jobs on the beach side, and in those areas where all these rich white people congregated, that's where most of us worked. And of course, a lot of the poor whites from the west side of the railroad tracks worked over there too. We all worked together.

There were no special arrangements to keep the races separated. We were just the help. We used the same bathrooms, and ate together in the same employee/staff dining room. It was a matter of survival: to have a job we were forced to come in close contact with each other. A lot of good came out of this because some relationships spread out into the community. This situation, and the things the rich white people in Ormond did, also helped outside the city; the attitude and behaviors spread out into the county, especially the Halifax area.

By having to work with rich people, working around them and serving them, gave the blacks, as well as the whites, more information about each other and better understanding. We felt a little more important than some people of the same race in other cities. I know the blacks in Ormond felt superior to the blacks in Holly Hill and Daytona.

Holly Hill was very prejudiced because they didn't have the rich white clientele—Holly Hill did not have a beach. They were inland people, and the blacks there were not exposed to the same things we were in Ormond Beach.

Ormond Beach and New Smyrna Beach were the most progressive cities in Volusia County, Working and serving the rich people in the Ormond area during those years in the late 30s and 40s, and even the into the 50s, created a completely different type of atmosphere, and we had a better class of people, both black and white.

The greatest transition period took place in the 40s. That coupled with the war that started in 1941, and the influx of military personnel, especially WACs, helped to better race relations and it enhanced the economy, which helped everybody. Daytona Beach benefited from it.

In Daytona Beach with the development of Bethune College, and with the military coming in, Daytona was able to reach a much higher peak of liberalism than a lot of other cities in Florida.

Nineteen

Three Influential Women

There were three ladies who had a very inspiring part to play in my development. I consider them special ladies.

Larry Hyde

Larry Hyde was a good friend. I knew her for sixty some years. She was an educator in the public school systems, a librarian, and lover of young people. She dedicated her time, effort and finances to helping with daycares, especially at her church, St. Timothy's Episcopal Church in Daytona Beach.

She worked with a lot of organizations in the community. She was a wonderful person, always willing to help resolve the needs of others.

She was also a good friend of Mary McLeod Bethune, founder of Bethune Cookman College.

Mary McLeod Bethune

Mary McLeod Bethune was one of the most influential persons in Daytona Beach history, and even in United States history. She was a great contributor to the condition in Daytona Beach, not only for black people, but for everybody. She developed a number of national and international contacts. Daytona Beach benefitted greatly from her influence. Many things that happened for the good can be attributed to her efforts.

Mrs. Bethune was instrumental in the election of the first black mayor of Daytona Beach, the first black city bus driver, the first black policemen and sheriff's department employees, and first black mail carriers.

She was also very involved in bringing a federal housing program to the area for low-income families. She was instrumental in arranging for a training facility of the Women's Army Corps, (The WACs) in Daytona Beach during World War Two. They were all white. There were no black WACs. It is said that the City of Daytona Beach benefitted financially greatly from the income generated by the WACs' being in the Daytona Beach area. The federal government paid for them to be here. The city benefited. The hotels benefited. They shopped in stores. And we young kids who would shine shoes for a nickel or a dime made out real well. Having them here was a plus-plus for Daytona.

Mrs. Bethune was also a major cause of a veteran's hospital Welch Convalescent Hospital, a hospital for wounded military personnel being created here. There were also many barracks in the Welch vicinity, around the hospital. This area is just east of where Halifax Hospital is now. It was like a military compound. A lot of that stuff was left behind, because the Mary Karl Vocational School, a predecessor of Daytona Beach Community College (now Daytona State College), Embry Riddle Aeronautical University, Halifax Hospital, local social services organizations and many others used a lot of those old barracks for many years. There was quite a lot of activity going on around here, and it was Mrs. Bethune's connection with President Roosevelt and strong friendship with

Mrs. Eleanor Roosevelt which surely helped the positive development.

She pretty much created Bethune-Cookman College alone. Now it's Bethune-Cookman University. She worked very hard in the community to establish good race relations. Her work in that regard is still evident today, contrary to many other cities. Mary McLeod Bethune was an outstanding organizer, educator, and person with a big heart. She helped thousands and thousands of people. She is one person that I had the opportunity to meet and talk with on many occasions. She would visit high school classrooms, and I met her as a high school student. Later on, I had the opportunity to take study trade at the college one summer. She constantly encouraged and counseled all students on how to be better.

She was a wonderful lady. There are many other things that she accomplished that history will record.

Daytona Beach had a good relationship with the major newspaper, the Daytona Beach News-Journal, where, once a week, they were given a whole page to write about activities in the black community. We also had a black editor for that page. She and her husband, Job Harrison, were leading political figures in the black community.

When Jackie Robinson was here practicing for the Montreal Baseball team, he lived in her house.

Daytona Beach was moving forward and Mrs. Bethune was one of the main persons to help it along. She was responsible for creating the type of atmosphere in Daytona Beach that made it conducive for Jackie Robinson to come here. He didn't have any incidents here. Daytona received him. It was just the other places that he went where he was not welcome, like Sanford and Jacksonville. She had created quite a relationship with whites in this community. She was highly respected. I have to give her credit for many of the good things that happened in Daytona Beach.

Mrs. Bethune invited Joe Lewis to come and visit the campus. He frequently stayed at a guest house on Campbell Street, now Martin Luther King Boulevard, which was attached to a nice restaurant called Little Gipsy Tea Room, all operated by Blacks. That's where all black stars and traveling professionals would often stay. They couldn't stay on the beachside even if they entertained over there. I'd heard Joe Lewis was at the Little Gipsy Tea Room while I was a student at Campbell High School. I had an old car to get from Ormond to school. On my lunch break, I went down to see Joe Lewis. I got a chance to meet him and talk to him, and I invited him to our school. He said he had an appointment with Mrs. Bethune. I offered him a ride, and took him to the college. I went in and said, "Joe Lewis is out in the car."

Everybody came out to greet him and take him in. I got in my little sub-standard Chevy and went back to school and I told my classmates what had happened, they all laughed. Then, they all wanted to see him before he left town.

I used to get a kick out of seeing Mrs. Bethune come into the classes while I was enrolled in the trade school. NYA was a program for young people who were from low-income families. They could go and learn a trade, and it didn't cost them anything. In fact the students were paid to learn a trade. It wasn't very much. I think it was about ten or twelve dollars a month. But you got to learn a free trade, to become a carpenter, auto mechanic, radio repairman (this was before television), tailoring and dry-cleaning. She would visit the vocational school quite often. She'd come right up to you and talk to you. If you dropped your head, she'd insist on your raising your head and looking eyeball to eyeball. "Stand up straight. " She was quite a person–quite a character. She was very unusual in that respect. I could write a book about her alone.

In my opinion, Mrs. Bethune was the catalyst for moving Daytona ahead in race relations more so than anybody or any one thing because she had the ear of white politicians, white law enforcement, and the white judiciary. Her girls, her students, shopped on Beach Street, the main shopping area. They had to be well dressed–they all wore a uniform and acted in a dignified manner.

Her students and the staff were highly respected by both the black and white communities. Bethune-Cookman was one of the great contributors as to the social, economic and respectable condition that prevailed in Daytona.

It was a beautiful thing to see how Bethune-Cookman set the pace for how a lot of things happened, including the local churches in the black community. Mrs. Bethune had her students dress up to attend church on Sunday afternoon. At 3 o'clock, they marched into chapel. It was a beautiful thing to see. People from the community came to observe the line on Sunday afternoon, and they were invited to join in. When the locals finished their own services at the different churches in the community, most of them would join in for the 3 o'clock service. Mrs. Bethune had local ministers participate and of course she would have her input. It was something that we looked forward to each Sunday.

Other things occurring on the Bethune-Cookman college campus helped the community. Keiser Practices was a small public/private school, available for first graders and elementary kids to attend, and this was where student teachers would more or less come to practice teaching. Keiser Practice was designed so that the graduates from Bethune-Cookman could teach youngsters and practice under the supervision of the professors and teachers. It helped the students get a better and a higher standard of training, and it also gave the teachers and students group practice under supervision, so they would be better teachers when they graduated. Many schools looked forward to receiving the graduate students from Bethune-Cookman College because they were so well trained and respected.

Blacks were treated better and had better positions in the two major cities in Florida at that time, Daytona Beach and West Palm Beach, than any other cities.

They experienced pretty much the same things with the influx of the northern big money coming into the area. Even today, Palm Beach is a mecca for the rich, and blacks who live Palm Beach pretty much followed the same trend as Ormond Beach. That is the blacks had a chance to go across the waterway and work on the beach for rich people and were exposed to, and learned from some of the things that they saw, heard and experienced. What rubbed off on them in Palm Beach they took back across the waterway to West Palm Beach. They not only made better salaries than some blacks in other locales, but they started investing and helping themselves, so West Palm Beach became the second best city to Daytona Beach as far as progress for blacks.

I must add a personal note here about my contribution to the Civil Rights Movement in the 60s. As a community leader, I organized a sit-in at the F. W. Woolworth's on Beach Street in Daytona. A large group of black men, me included, walked into the store and took our places at the lunch counter. The store was fairly empty at the time, so nobody paid us much attention. We decided we'd sit there all day. A young waitress came out from the kitchen and began taking our orders. What a surprise that was. Took the wind right out of our sails. A few minutes later, though, her manager came out and said, "I'm sorry, gentlemen, it is our corporate policy that we can't serve you. I'm sorry."

We all looked at one another, but no one moved. We remained in our seats all day. No one came in. No one confronted us. Eventually, toward the end of the day, we just drifted off home without even a newspaper reporter noting that we'd been there.

Marietta Dowdell Daniels

Marietta Dowdell Daniels

My favorite lady was Marietta Dowdell Daniels. She was the mother of thirteen children. She was unfortunate enough to start raising them during the deep depression of the 1920s. President Hoover was the president at the time. She was able to keep the children fed and clothed in the most adverse circumstances. She is always in my thoughts.

One summer on the plantation, my mother had a young baby, who she'd take to the fields and set a place for him on the ground to sleep. This one day, she came home to the shack that was our home to cook the evening meal for her family. She made a fire in the cook stove and as she sweated in the hot kitchen trying to prepare the meal, she had the baby sitting on a blanket on the floor. The baby crawled over to the stove, reached up and grabbed that red-hot stove. The baby's tender hands just stuck to the stove. The baby cried out. My mother turned, horrified and pulled the baby away, leaving quite a bit of flesh from his hand on that door. This was very disturbing for my mother, but she performed the only kind of first aid she knew. She put butter on the burned hands, thinking that was the best way to take care of it. When the family came home, she explained what had happened. We all knew immediately when we walked in because we could smell the seared flesh that had sizzled on that red-hot old wooden stove. They did the best they could to try to ease the pain. We all remember that night, because the baby cried all night in pain. The whole family stayed awake.

The next day, they finally got permission from the boss of the plantation to seek medical attention. They took the baby on down to town to a doctor. The doctor made the mistake of treating it with a lot of Vaseline or something similar and wrapped it up. He gave the family some pain tablets to be crushed up and spooned up with water for the baby. As time went on, our mother kept working on the helping the baby heal. Somebody convinced her to remove the cloth from the baby's hands so the skin could breathe. She did that; the hands let off a strong odor. Our mother kept putting an oil, or paste or salve, but it didn't seem to be getting any better. She was staying home and a lot of the other family members weren't working so well because nobody was getting a good night's sleep.

The plantation boss suggested they cut the hand off because it was not reparable. He said she should stay in the house and meet the veterinarian to cut off the hand. He was supposed to come out to the house at about 9 or 10 in the morning. But this did not meet with our mother's approval. So she took the baby and some items to survive on, and went out and hid in the fields until the vet came and left. The plantation boss was not pleased about that. Our mother said she would not let the hand be removed. She stood up to them all.

She said her child would not lose that hand. Whatever was left of the hand, she'd help the child.

Fortunately, some people came through, some gypsies, in wagons. They'd stop, asking for water and other things. They saw the baby and gave my mother some good advice and some medication to apply to the hand. The hand started to improve. Everybody was happy. I applaud my mother for her bravery. I think she was one of the most wonderful ladies in the world.

I applaud these three ladies, and I'm sure if any of them ever had to do her life over again, it would not change very much.

Twenty

My Accident

One morning not so long ago I was crossing the street in front of Daytona Beach Florida City Hall. I was a victim of a hit and run driver. I was just lucky that there were people there to assist me. I'm sure thankful to Dr. Staley and his great staff at Florida Health Care, Amy, Jackie, DiDi and the orthopedic group and of course Dave and his partners at Ability Rehab. My buddy Scott and Charles and the staff at Progressive Physical Therapy Center. Quite grateful to my friends at Florida Health Care: Karen and Jackie, Kristin, Kara, Bunny, Laura, and Chip and Hugh, Christine, Loretta, JoAnn, Kathy, RoseAnn, Flo, Carol, Connie, Stacey, Nora, Frank, and Wayne. My family was instrumental in helping me get through my time of incapacitation. Miss Hyde, Harriett, Merle and Doreen, Janet, Dee, and others.

I was fortunate and grateful to have a caring family. And Lily, Shara, Destiny, Bernice, Jo, Iola, and Geneva, Susan, John, Helen, the Brennons and my son, James Derek. They were instrumental in helping me with the healing process and to them I am grateful.

Twenty-One

Revisiting the Past

I continued to do things to help the community all my working life. After many years of working with community projects, and sharing in business ventures, restaurants and real estate, I finally decided to retire. I had had twelve years of schooling, four years of college education in Tallahassee, and been gainfully employed in different venues. When I was comfortably retired in my comfortable home, with its four bedrooms, Florida room, and all the other extras, I thought about the plantation where I had worked as a young boy, and decided to visit our old home place and see just what had happened since my departure.

It was amazing to see that the plantation where I, along with a hundred or more black workers, used to pick cotton, nut grass and beans, shake peanuts, cut sorghum cane, and do all of the farming chores. Now, not a common laborer, a migrant worker, or a farm hand was to be seen. The huge plantation only had one employee, one person—a man who operated a great big old machine, which did all the cultivation, all the seed planting for the crop and everything else. I'm sure that during harvest time, one machine would perform all the picking too.

I tried to pick out exactly where the little shanty that we used to live in had stood. I could not find the exact spot because all of the shanties had been torn down. Everything had changed. The well that my forefathers and I used to drink from had been covered up. Instead of drawing water from the well like we used to, the farm now has pumps and an irrigation system. All they have to do is flip a switch and the crops get watered. The ditch that used to run alongside of the road was filled in with a pipe underneath for the drainage. The dirt road that we used to travel on is now all asphalt. There are telephone poles, and electrical poles along the way. Electric lights have replaced the kerosene lamps that we used, and there's no longer a commissary to purchase kerosene and everything else we needed.

There was only one thing we did not get from the commissary. Every week or two we were able to buy a block of ice when my parents went in to town. That was a delicacy, ice. Pure ice. We wrapped it up tight in a burlap sack and put it in the icebox. We kept it real tightly sealed until the next Sunday when we could have lemonade. That day we would just have a real good time, eating fried chicken, which was a popular dish for Sunday dinner, and drinking lemonade.

Anyway, back then, with no electricity and no refrigeration when we had no ice in the icebox, if it was cool enough outside, we'd wrap up leftovers and set the package on the little counter top on the back porch so it would keep cool. We'd light a fire in the old wood stove to warm up whatever we needed.

Despite all the changes made over the years, evidence of where we used to live still exists. I mentioned earlier about the outhouses in Cordele, and how we moved them from place to place as the pits filled. Now you can see exactly where they were because the vegetation is conspicuously taller and lusher in those spots. As I drove around that plantation, I saw those spots and knew the shanties used to stand not far from the line of outhouses, the only evidence of our existence. The whole plantation had been completely reconfigured to suit the combine operation of the machinery. There is no more need for cotton pickers; that one machine picked it all; the driver controlled the entire operation all by himself sitting in an air conditioned cab.

I went into town in search of The Bottom, a little store that had operated for blacks by a big man named Riley Robinson. It was gone, replaced by a housing development. The three five and ten cent stores that used to be along the avenue down the main section of town are no longer there.

All of those things have changed since the days I lived there. Following my visit to the area, I learned that memories still sit in a lot of the older people. The younger people never had to experience the negative, bad things the older generation did. It may sound strange to some, but we were happy in our situation because we were ignorant of other things that were better; we were ignorant of that fact there was a better life.

The people in the county have changed. When I walk down through those same streets that I walked many, many years ago, I relive those days. I have a feeling. But now I can walk into those stores, and I don't see any of those No Colored signs over the water fountain. There's no back door to any of the stores other than for delivery people. Now I can use the front door. The counters where we were unable to sit are now occupied by all people. There are about as many black servers and cooks as white. Now I am treated with respect as a customer.

Cordele, Crisp County, Georgia, will never be that town I grew up in again, and I'm grateful for that.

What a change from a one bedroom shack where mother and father and the two little ones slept in the living room, our parents in the bed and the two youngest ones on a pallet on the floor beside them with the other eight of us larger kids on pallets in the bedroom.

Twenty-Two

Full Circle

Today I'm retired, living in a comfortable home in Daytona Beach. My beautiful Carrie has passed on.

On Saturdays I open my garage where I collect clothing and food. Folks all around the area know they can come for free food and clothing. Some shops donate their day old baked goods to my efforts. I am happy, healthy and handsome.

"I've been called a niggerlet, colored, Negro, black, and African-American. Now, I want to come full term in my metamorphosis, and to be a person without reference to my race. But, if I have to have a label, I prefer black." - James F. Daniels